FRESH & TASTY

Chicken

R&R PUBLICATIONS MARKETING PTY LTD

Published by:
R&R Publications Marketing Pty. Ltd
ACN 083 612 579
PO Box 254, Carlton North, Victoria 3054 Australia
Phone (61 3) 9381 2199 Fax (61 3) 9381 2689
Australia wide toll free 1800 063 296
E-mail: richardc@bigpond.net.au

Fresh & Tasty Chicken

Publisher: Richard Carroll
Creative Director: Lucy Adams
Production Manager: Anthony Carroll
Food Photography: Steve Baxter, Phillip Wilkins, David Munns, Thomas Odulate, Christine Hanscomb
and Frank Wieder
Home economist: Sara Buenfeld, Emma Patmore, Nancy McDougall, Louise Pickford, Jane Stevenson,
Oded Schwartz, Alison Austin and Jane Lawrie
Food Stylists: Helen Payne, Sue Russell, Sam Scott, Antonia Gaunt and Oded Schwartz
Recipe Development: Terry Farris, Jacqueline Bellefontaine, Becky Johnson, Valerie Barrett, Emma
Patmore, Geri Richards, Pam Mallender and Ellen Argyriou
Nutritional Consultant: Moya de Wet BSc SRD
Proof Reader: Paul Hassing

Includes Index
ISBN 1 740222 37 7
EAN 9 781740 222 372

First Edition Printed September 2002
Computer Typeset in Adobe Garamond
Printed in Singapore

Contents

Introduction 4

Chicken in a Crust 9

Chicken on a Grill 21

Chicken in a Salad 29

Chicken in a Pan 43

Chicken in an Oven 59

Glossary 76

Weights and Measures 78

Index 80

Introduction

Chicken has always been a valuable food source. From the earliest recorded history, it has appeared on the tables of ancient Egypt, Greece, Rome and Asia.

The ancestor of the chicken of today is thought to be the Indian Jungle Fowl which was domesticated by the Indus Valley civilisation in about 2500 BC. It's not known how the bird travelled to other areas, but travel it did. The chicken has been used by almost all cultures throughout the world - each adding aspects of their culinary heritage to this versatile meat.

With this rich diversity of cultures, our repertoire of chicken dishes has expanded to new dimensions. Ethnic dishes from other countries, such as Tandoori Chicken, Chicken Cacciatore and Hawaiian Chicken, are just as popular in the world as the traditional roast chicken.

Through the pages of this book you will experience the new flavor combinations which have resulted from our culinary cultural exchange, presented in simple and quick-to-prepare recipes.

Chicken production today has made available not only the bird dressed and ready for the pot, but also each cut portioned out so you can buy as you need. Gone are the days when the favourite part of the family chicken, usually the breast, was the most popular piece.

Nutritional Value

Chicken is high in first class protein, which means it has of the essential amino acids. Vitamins, particularly A and the B group, are well represented, as are minerals including iron and zinc. It is a light, tender meat which makes it easy to chew and digest, so it is especially suitable for infants, children and the elderly. With the skin removed, chicken is even lower in fat, making it an ideal food for everyone.

Purchasing and Storage of Chicken

Chicken can be purchased fresh or frozen, whole or in pieces. The choice is yours, depending how and when you wish to prepare and eat the chicken.

Fresh Chicken

- When buying fresh chicken, make it the last purchase on your shopping trip. It's advisable to take an insulated bag to place the chicken in to keep it cold on the trip home.
- On arriving home with your chicken purchase, remove it from the package (if any), rinse it and wipe it dry with a paper towel. Cover it loosely with plastic wrap and refrigerate immediately. Fresh chicken may be kept in the refrigerator for 3 days. Place it in the coldest part of the refrigerator, below 4°C/39°F.
- If chicken needs to be stored longer, it's better to buy ready frozen chicken than to buy it fresh and freeze it at home.
- If chicken pieces are to be purchased and frozen for future use, make sure they're are fresh. Wipe them dry with paper towel, then pack them flat in plastic freezer bags. Remove air by pushing it towards the opening and tape the bag closed. Label and date the packages.

Frozen Chicken

- When purchasing frozen chicken, check that the packages are not torn.
- Place them in the freezer immediately you return home.
- Thaw frozen chicken thoroughly before cooking to avoid toughening the texture and to reduce the chance of undercooking. Undercooked parts can harbour food-spoiling bacteria.
- Don't refreeze thawed chicken. It is advisable to cook thawed chicken and freeze it when cooked.
- To thaw frozen chicken, remove the wrap, place it on a rack in a dish to allow the liquid to collect beneath the chicken. Don't touch it. Cover loosely with fresh plastic wrap and place it in the refrigerator for 24 hours. This is the safest way to thaw. Thawing on the kitchen bench encourages bacteria growth and should be avoided.

Preparation

There are simple rules for the preparation and handling of chicken. Adhering to these rules will lessen the likelihood of bacterial growth and thereby increase the quality, flavour and enjoyment of your dishes. Many of these rules apply to other perishable foods and should become a common part of your kitchen routine.

Food producers and retailers maintain high standards of quality and cleanliness so that we can buy safe and wholesome foods with confidence. Consumers need to maintain these quality and safety standards after purchase. Perishable foods, like chicken, need special attention to prevent deterioration and possible food poisoning.

The tips below should be employed to avoid bacterial growth and transfer.

Safe Food Handling Tips

- Wash your hands thoroughly before handling fresh chicken. Wash them again before handling other food.
- Chopping boards, knives and other utensils must be washed with hot soapy water after handling raw chicken and other raw foods to prevent cross-contamination .
- Always keep cold food at 4°C/39°F or below in a refrigerator.
- Never keep raw chicken at room temperature for longer than 1 hour, including preparation time.
- Poultry must be cooked through to the centre, not left rare. This ensures that all bacteria have been killed by the heat penetration. To test, insert a skewer into the centre of the chicken or portion - if the juice runs clear, the chicken is cooked through.
- Stuffing should be treated with special care as bacteria from raw poultry can grow in it. Stuff loosely, only $^2/_3$ full, just before cooking and remove the stuffing immediately after cooking.
- Cool cooked foods quickly by placing them in the refrigerator. Don't be afraid, the refrigerator is built to take them.

- Large quantities of food should be divided into smaller portions to allow quicker cooking. This relates particularly to simmered chicken and chicken stock. Do not be afraid to place hot foods in the refrigerator - it is built to take them.
- Store raw and cooked foods separately, with cooked foods at the top and raw foods at the bottom on a tray or plate. Don't let juices drop onto other foods.
- The danger zone for bacterial growth is between 4°C/39°F and 65°C/149°F, so keep foods below or above this range. Food must not be left to stand on the kitchen bench, as room temperature is in the danger zone.
- When reheating cooked chicken, bring it to 75°C/167°F and hold it there for a few minutes.

Tips for Cooking Chicken in the Microwave

Whole Chicken

- The microwave does not brown chicken as a conventional oven does, but a brown appearance can be achieved by either rubbing the surface with paprika or brushing it with a glaze.
- Tie the legs together with string or an elastic band to give a more even cooking shape.
- Calculate cooking time simply by doubling the size number on the chicken (e.g. a No. 15 is cooked for 30 minutes) and cook on MEDIUM/HIGH. Larger chickens are bestcooked on MEDIUM/HIGH for the first half of the cooking time, then on MEDIUM for the remainder, adding 5–8 minutes cooking time per 1 kg/2¼ lb.
- Remember the starting temperature of the chicken will affect cooking time. A refrigerated chicken will take a few minutes longer than one at room temperature. It is advisable to cook the chicken on HIGH for the first 3–5 minutes to warm the surface, then MEDIUM/HIGH for remainder of the cooking time.

Chicken Pieces

- For even cooking arrange chicken pieces with the thicker part to the outside of the dish or roasting rack
- Halfway through cooking, rearrange pieces in the centre to the outside
- Chicken casseroles cook better if the chicken is cut into small even pieces so cut breasts into 2 pieces and separate thighs from drumsticks.
- Chicken pieces may be browned in a browning dish before adding to a casserole, or browned in a frying pan before microwaving. You may prefer to remove the skin before placing chicken in a casserole as they tend to become rubbery.
- Chicken pieces can be crumbed then cooked on a roasting rack with pleasing results. Choose a deep-coloured dried bread crumb and add dried herbs, lemon, pepper or toasted sesame seeds. The crumbs will remain crisp.

Chicken in a Crust

No matter how you roll, flan or skewer it, the versatility of chicken never fails to surprise. Wrapped in filo, puff pastry, pitta or tortilla, these dishes carry messages of delight from Greece, Italy, India, Mexico and the Middle East. Good things come in small packages, especially when they're pasties, triangles, foccaccias and burritos. Don't be surprised to find yourself doubling the ingredients to enjoy these light meals as main courses.

Middle Eastern Chicken Pasties

**1 quantity Ricotta Pastry
milk**

Chicken and Vegetable Filling
1 tsp olive oil
1 small red onion, diced
1 stalk celery, diced
1 tsp ground cumin
$^1/_2$ tsp dry mustard
**$1^1/_4$ cups skinless shredded
cooked chicken**
**$^1/_2$ cup grated zucchini or
chopped green capsicum**
**$^1/_2$ cup additional vegetables
of your choice
(e.g. chopped spinach
or grated pumpkin)**
2 tbsp currants or sultanas
**1 tbsp chopped fresh parsley
or oregano**
**$^1/_4$ cup low-fat natural
yoghurt**
1 tbsp chutney
2 tbsp couscous
1 tsp grated lemon zest
2 tsp lemon juice

Ricotta Pastry
2 cups self-raising flour
$^1/_2$ cup low-fat ricotta cheese
$^1/_2$ cup buttermilk
1 egg white
2 tbsp unsaturated oil
**1–2 tbsp chilled
skim milk**

1 *Filling:* Heat the oil in a
nonstick frying pan over a
medium heat. Add the onion,
celery, cumin and mustard.
Cook, stirring, for 2–3 minutes
or until soft and fragrant.

2 Add the chicken, zucchini,
additional vegetables, currants,
parsley, yoghurt and chutney.
Cook, stirring occasionally, for
5–7 minutes. Remove the pan
from the heat. Stir in the
couscous, lemon zest and
lemon juice. Cool.
3 Preheat the oven. Lightly
spray or brush a baking tray
with unsaturated oil or line
with nonstick baking paper.
4 To assemble, roll out the
pastry to 2mm/$^1/_8$in thick and,
using a bread and butter plate as
a guide, cut out 4 rounds. Place
$^1/_4$ of the filling on 1 half of each
round, leaving a 1cm/$^1/_2$in
border around the edge. Brush
the edge with milk or water.
Fold the uncovered half over the
filling, pressing the edges to seal.
Using a fork, prick the pastry
several times. Place on a
prepared baking tray. Brush with
milk. Bake for 20 minutes or
until the pastry is crisp and
golden.

Ricotta Pastry
1 Place the flour, ricotta
cheese, buttermilk, egg white
and oil in a food processor.
Using the pulse button, process
until just combined.
2 With the machine running,
slowly add the skim milk until
the mixture forms a dough.
3 Turn the pastry onto a
lightly floured surface. Knead
into a ball. Wrap the pastry in
plastic food wrap. Refrigerate
for at least 30 minutes or until
ready to use. Makes enough to
cover a 20cm/8in round pie.

Makes 4 pasties
Preparation 20mins
Cooking 30mins
Calories 549 per pastie
Fat 18g

OVEN TEMPERATURE
190°C, 370°F, GAS 5

Chicken and Almond Triangles

1 tbsp olive oil
¹/₂ cup slivered almonds
1 medium onion, finely chopped
¹/₂ tsp salt
1 tsp ground cinnamon
1 tsp paprika
2 tsp ground cumin
455g/1 lb minced chicken meat
2 small tomatoes, chopped
¹/₄ cup raisins, chopped
**2 tbsp finely chopped Italian
parsley**
¹/₄ cup dry white wine
1 packet filo pastry
canola oil spray

1 Heat the oil in a frying pan and sauté the almonds until pale gold in colour. Quickly remove with a slotted spoon and drain on paper towel. Add the onion and fry until soft, stir in the salt and spices and cook until aromatic. Add the minced chicken and stirfry until almost cooked. Add the tomatoes, raisins, parsley, almonds and wine and simmer, covered, 15 minutes.

Uncover and cook until the juices are absorbed. Allow to cool.
2 Thaw the pastry according to packet instructions. Count out 14 sheets, repack and refreeze the remainder. Position the pastry with the long side parallel to bench edge in front of you. Cut it into 3 x 15cm/6in wide strips. Stack and cover with clean tea towel. Taking 2 strips at a time, spray each lightly with canola oil spray and fold in half, long side to long side. Spray the surface with oil spray.
3 Place a teaspoon of filling on the bottom end of each strips. Fold the right-hand corner over to form a triangle then fold on the straight then on the diagonal until end is reached. Repeat with remaining. Place on a tray sprayed with oil. Spray the tops of the triangles with oil and bake in a preheated moderate oven for 20–25 minutes. Serve hot as finger food.
Variation: 225g/¹/₂ lb chicken stirfry fried with 1 chopped onion, cooled and mixed into 225g/¹/₂ lb ricotta cheese and 1 beaten egg.

Makes 42
Preparation 15mins
Cooking 45mins
Calories 44
Fat 0.2g

Chicken and Prune Roll

OVEN TEMPERATURE
200°C, 400°F, GAS 6

Serves 6-8
Preparation 10mins
Cooking 40mins
Calories 184
Fat 1g

**2 rashers of bacon, trimmed
of fat and finely chopped
1 medium onion, finely chopped
10 pitted prunes
455g/1 lb minced chicken meat
2 tbsp dried breadcrumbs
¹/₂ tsp each salt & pepper
1 tsp cumin
1 egg, lightly beaten
1 sheet frozen puff pastry
1 tbsp milk
2 tsp poppy seeds**

1 Place the bacon and onion in a small heated pan and cook while stirring for 1 minute. Chop 5 prunes finely; add to the minced chicken along with the breadcrumbs, seasonings, egg and bacon/onion mixture. Mix well to distribute the ingredients.
2 Line a flat oven tray with a sheet of baking paper or foil and place a sheet of thawed puff pastry onto the tray.

Spoon ¹/₂ of the meat mixture along the centre of the sheet in an even strip about 8cm/3in wide and to the edge of the pastry at both ends. Arrange the 5 remaining whole prunes along the centre then cover with the remaining minced chicken and smooth to even thickness.
3 Brush the back strip of pastry with water, lift the front pastry over the meat and lift the back pastry to overlap the front. Press lightly along the seam to seal. Lift the paper and turn the meat, roll over to rest on the seam join, then pull the paper to bring it into the centre of the tray. Trim off any paper overhang. Glaze the roll with milk and sprinkle with poppy seeds.
4 Bake in a preheated hot oven for 15 minutes then turn oven down to 180°C/350°F/Gas 4 and continue cooking for 25 minutes until golden. Serve with vegetable accompaniments

Chicken Focaccia with Marinated Vegetables

**500g/1 lb chicken breast
fillets (skin off)
1 clove garlic, crushed
salt and pepper
1 tbsp lemon juice
2 tsp olive oil
6 portions of focaccia bread
(individual or slab)
1 tbsp olive oil extra
6 slices marinated roasted eggplant
85g/3oz marinated mushrooms
6 slices marinated roasted
red capsicum**

1   Trim the breast fillets. Place in a glass dish and add garlic, seasonings, lemon juice and oil. Cover and marinate for 30 minutes in the refrigerator.

Heat a non-stick pan or greased griddle-plate, sear the fillets 1 minute each side, then cook for 3 minutes each side or until cooked through. When cooked, cut into diagonal slices. Keep hot.

2   Cut the focaccia slab into serving portions and split through the centre. Split the individual breads if using. Brush cut surfaces with olive oil.

3   Place a slice of eggplant on each base, arrange the chicken slices on top and cover with mushrooms and capsicum. Replace the top slices. Place in a moderate oven for 10 minutes. Serve hot with marinated vegetables as a light meal.

OVEN TEMPERATURE
160°C, 325°F, GAS 3

Makes 5 sandwiches
Preparation 10mins
plus marinating
Cooking 18mins
Calories 349
Fat 1g

Chicken Leek and Mushroom Flan

OVEN TEMPERATURE
180°C, 350°F, GAS 4

*Tip: Pie can be
frozen for future use.*

Serves 4-6
Preparation 10mins
Cooking 55mins
Calories 498
Fat 5.5g

2 frozen savoury pie flan
455g/1 lb chicken breast fillets
(skin off)
1 tbsp canola oil
2 leeks, trimmed and thinly sliced
salt and pepper
200g/7oz button mushrooms,
sliced
1 tbsp lemon juice
45g/1$^{1}/_{2}$ oz packet cream of chicken
soup, salt-reduced
1 cup water
1 cup milk
2 eggs, beaten
$^{1}/_{4}$ tsp nutmeg
85g/3oz flaked almonds

1 Preheat the oven. Place the frozen pie flans on an oven tray and blind bake for 10–15 minutes as directed on the packet.
2 Slice the chicken breasts with a large knife at a 45° angle into 1cm/$^{1}/_{2}$ in-thick slices.

3 Heat the oil in a large pan and cook the leeks until soft. Push them to the side of the pan, add the chicken and cook for 1 minute on each side. Sprinkle lightly with salt and pepper, add the mushrooms and lemon juice, turn down heat and simmer for 3 minutes.
4 Make the soup to packet directions using 1 cup of water and 1 cup of milk. When boiling and thick, remove from the heat and cool slightly. Quickly stir in the eggs and nutmeg.
5 Fill the 2 pie flans with the chicken, mushrooms and leeks and stir any juices into the sauce. Spoon the sauce over the chicken filling, dividing equally between the two. Sprinkle each pie with $^{1}/_{2}$ the almonds to make a dense covering. Bake in a oven for 25–30 minutes until filling is set. Serve with a tossed salad.

Chicken Pitta

900g/2 lb chicken thighs
2 cups water
$^{1}/_{2}$ tsp salt
$^{1}/_{2}$ tsp chicken stock powder
455g/1 lb onions (4 large), chopped
2 tbsp butter
75g/2$^{1}/_{2}$oz grated Romano or Parmesan cheese
$^{1}/_{4}$ tsp nutmeg
$^{1}/_{2}$ tsp freshly ground black pepper
4 eggs, beaten
canola oil spray
1 packet filo pastry

1 Place thighs in a saucepan and add the water and salt. Bring slowly to the boil; skim off the froth as it rises. When the water is clear, add the stock powder and onions.

Cover and simmer for 30–35 minutes until the chicken is tender. Remove the chicken to a plate. Continue to simmer the onions uncovered until they become soft and the water has reduced. It should look like a pulpy, runny sauce.

2 Cut the chicken into strips and return to the saucepan. Add the butter and simmer for 2 minutes, stirring occasionally. Remove from the heat and allow to cool slightly. Stir to release trapped heat. When cool, stir in the cheese, nutmeg, pepper and eggs.

3 Spray the base and sides of a baking dish, approximately 28cm x 24cm x 5cm/11in x 10in x 2in, (metal cooks best) with canola oil spray and line it with a sheet of filo pastry. Spray the filo with canola spray,

moving in a zig-zag pattern to cover all areas. Place a second sheet on top. Spray, then continue until 8 sheets are placed.

4 Pour in the chicken mixture, and fold overlapping edges over the filling. Cover the top with 8 sheets of filo and spray with canola spray as before. Trim the edges, allowing a slight overhang. With the tip of a sharp knife, lightly score the top 2 sheets into squares to make cutting easier when the pie is cooked. Wet your hand and splash the top of pie with water. Place in a preheated oven and bake for 45 minutes, until puffed and golden. Remove from the oven and rest for 10 minutes before cutting through the score marks. Serve hot or cold

Oven temperature
180°C, 350°F, Gas 4

Serves 8
Preparation 20mins
Cooking 90mins
Calories 295
Fat 5.8g

Curried Chicken Rolls

OVEN TEMPERATURE
190°C, 370°F, GAS 5

Tip: Can be made in advance and reheated in a moderate oven.

Serves 16–20
Preparation 15mins
Cooking 25mins
Calories 62
Fat 0.3g

2 tsp canola oil
1 medium onion, finely chopped
1 small clove garlic, crushed
2 tsp mild curry paste
$1^1/_2$ tbsp lemon juice
455g/1 lb minced chicken meat
3 tbsp dried breadcrumbs
$^1/_2$ tsp salt
$^1/_2$ tsp pepper
2 tbsp chopped fresh coriander
2 sheets frozen puff pastry
1 tbsp milk for glazing
1 tbsp sesame seeds

1 Heat the oil in a small pan, add the onion and garlic and fry until onion is soft. Stir in the curry paste and cook a little. Add the lemon juice and stir to mix.
Set aside.

Combine the minced chicken, breadcrumbs, salt, pepper and coriander and add the onion/curry mixture. Mix well.

2 Place a thawed sheet of puff pastry on a work surface and cut in half across the centre. Pile $^1/_4$ of the meat mixture in a thick $1^1/_2$cm/$^1/_2$in wide strip along the centre of the strip. Brush the exposed pastry at the back with water, lift the front strip of pastry over the filling and roll to rest onto the back strip. Press lightly to seal. Cut the roll into 4–5 equal portions. Repeat with the second half and then with the second sheet. Glaze with milk and sprinkle with sesame seeds. Place onto a flat baking tray.

3 Cook in a preheated hot oven for 10 minutes, reduce heat to 180°C/350°F/Gas 4 and continue cooking for 15 minutes until golden brown. Serve hot as finger food.

Lavash Rolls

canola oil spray
900g/2 lb chicken tenderloins
8 pieces lavash flat bread
315g/11oz mayonnaise
1 small lettuce, shredded
$^1/_2$ bunch spring onions, chopped
4 tomatoes, sliced
1 tub hummus
2 tbsp lemon juice
salt and pepper

1 Spray a heated non-stick pan or griddle plate with oil spray and cook the tenderloins for 2 minutes on each side.
2 Place each lavash sheet on a work surface. Spread lightly with mayonnaise. Sprinkle with lettuce leaving the bottom 4cm/1$^1/_2$ in uncovered. Sprinkle spring onions over the lettuce and place on tomato slices. Place 3–4 tenderloins down the centre and drizzle with a little hummus thinned with lemon juice.
3 Turn up the bottom edge to hold in the filling and roll from the side into a tight roll. Wrap the bottom half in greaseproof paper or foil and serve.

Note: Quantities given are for 8 rolls. Make adjustments for number required. Other salad vegetables and fruit may be used according to preference, eg: avocado, grated carrot, celery, pineapple, nuts, etc.

Serves 8
Preparation 8mins
Cooking 6mins
Calories 395
Fat 2.3g

No-Fuss Chicken Party Sticks

OVEN TEMPERATURE
180°C, 350°F, GAS 4

Makes 32
Preparation 30mins
Cooking 30mins
Calories 309
Fat 3g

900g/2 lb chicken tenderloins
salt and pepper
1¹/₃ kg/3 lb packet frozen puff
pastry
1 quantity spicy satay sauce
or sweet chilli sauce
1 tbsp poppy seeds
or sesame seeds

Spicy Satay Sauce
³/₄ cup peanut butter
³/₄ cup water
2 tbsp brown sugar
¹/₈ tsp chilli powder, or to taste
1 tbsp soy sauce
1 tbsp grated onion
2 tbsp toasted sesame seeds
bamboo skewers, soaked

1 Sprinkle the salt and pepper over the tenderlions. Cut a sheet of thawed pastry into 4 squares. Place a tenderloin on each square and add a dash of sauce. Roll up either on the straight or on the diagonal, leaving the ends open. Place seam-side down on a flat oven tray and glaze with milk or egg wash. Sprinkle with poppy seeds or sesame seeds.

2 Bake in a preheated moderate oven for 25–30 minutes. Serve hot as finger food with the same sauce used as a dipping sauce.

3 Mix all the satay sauce ingredients together in a saucepan, heat to a simmer. Keep on the heat for 5 minutes and allow to cool.

Spicy Chicken Burritos

900g/2 lb chicken stirfry
1 tbsp olive oil
1 large onion, finely chopped
1 clove garlic, crushed
185g/6$^{1}/_{2}$ oz Paul Newman's
Own Chunky Tomato, Onion
and Garlic Sauce (or packaged
sauce of choice)
$^{1}/_{2}$ tsp chilli powder

Toppings
1 tub guacamole
2 large onions, thinly sliced
$^{1}/_{2}$ carton sour cream
340g/12oz grated tasty
cheddar cheese
400g/14oz refried beans,
heated (optional)
12 Mexican tortillas

1 Chop the stirfry into smaller pieces. Heat the oil in a large frying pan.

Add the onion and garlic and fry until soft. Add the chicken and stir to brown it on all sides. Stir in the sauce and the chilli powder. Simmer for 15 minutes or until chicken is cooked.

2 Prepare the toppings and place in serving dishes. Heat the tortillas by the method on the pack. The preferred method is to heat a large frying pan and place in a tortilla. Heat the for 40 seconds each side, long enough to roast slightly. Remove and place in a clean towel and cover. Heat remainder and stack in the towel. Serve in the towel in a basket.

3 Invite each guest to make their own burrito by placing chicken mixture on the tortilla and adding their choice of toppings. Roll the buritto and enjoy.

Serves makes 12
Preparation 10mins
Cooking 20mins
Calories 306
Fat 3.5g

Chicken on a Grill

On a barbecue or grill, nothing cooks with the satisfying sear and savor of chicken. Here you'll find juicy kebabs, spicy brochettes and magical marinades to transport you overnight to China, Malaysia and the Deep South. Try these dishes soon. Your barbecue won't know what's hit it and you'll never look at plain old steamed rice and couscous in the same way again.

Citrus and Spice Grilled Chicken

Serves 2-3
Preparation 10mins
plus marinating
Cooking 35mins
Calories 313
Fat 1g

900g/2 lb chicken

Marinade
¹/₂ **cup cider vinegar**
¹/₂ **cup orange juice**
¹/₂ **cup grapefruit juice**
1 tsp cinnamon
¹/₂ **tsp ground nutmeg**
1 tsp sugar
¹/₂ **tsp salt (optional)**

1 Wash the chicken inside and out and pat dry with paper towels. With a cleaver or large, sharp knife, cut the chicken through the breastbone and open out. Cut on each side of the backbone and discard. (Can be used for stock)
2 Mix the marinade ingredients together.

Place the chicken halves in a non-metal dish and smother with the marinade. Cover and refrigerate for 12 hours or overnight, turning occasionally.
3 Heat the oven griller element or gas griller to medium. Place the chicken halves in the base of the grill pan under the grill. Cook for 10 minutes each side, brushing frequently with marinade.
4 Lift the chicken onto the grilling rack to closer to bring it closer to the heat and cook for 5 minutes each side. Turn the heat to high and cook about 2 minutes to brown and crisp. Remove the chicken to a heated platter.
5 Skim the fat from the pan juices and pour the juices over the chicken. Serve hot with vegetable accompaniments.

Southern Barbecued Chicken

**1³/₄ kg/4 lb fresh chicken,
cut into pieces**

Southern Barbecue Sauce
**340mL/12fl oz tomato puree
1 cup cider vinegar
¹/₂ cup canola oil
¹/₃ cup Worcestershire sauce
¹/₂ cup brown sugar
¹/₄ cup corn syrup or molasses
2 tbsp French-style mustard
2–3 cloves garlic, ground
¹/₄ cup lemon juice**

1 Prepare the Southern Barbecue Sauce in advance. Place all the ingredients into a stainless steel saucepan and stir to combine. Bring to a simmer and continue to simmer over low heat for 15–20 minutes, stirring regularly to prevent catching. Stand for 1 hour to cook and to allow the flavours to blend. Store in jars or bottles in the refrigerator (if not used immediately).

2 Cut the chicken into pieces. As a 1³/₄ kg/4 lb chicken is a large bird, the breast can be cut into 3–4 pieces each side. Heat the barbecue to moderate and oil the grill plate. Lightly sear the chicken pieces on all sides over a direct heat, about 4 minutes each side. Lift the chicken onto a plate.

3 Place 1¹/₂ cups of the sauce into a bowl and place by the barbecue. Place a sheet of baking paper over the grill bars and prick at intervals between the runs to allow ventilation. Replace the chicken onto the baking paper and brush well with the sauce.

4 Close the lid and cook for 10 minutes, then lift the lid, brush with sauce, turn the chicken, brush the underside with sauce, close lid and cook for 10 minutes. Repeat this process every 10 minutes for a total of 4–5 times or 40–50 minutes until the chicken is rich brown in colour and cooked through. If the chicken is cooking too quickly, reduce the heat by turning down the gas or raking the coals to the sides. Heat the extra sauce in a small saucepan on the barbecue.

5 Serve the chicken with the hot sauce and jacket potatoes cooked on the barbecue with the chicken. Accompany with a salad.

Serves 6–8
Preparation 30 mins
plus marinating
Cooking 30 mins
Calories 444
Fat 3.7 g

Grilled Sesame Chicken with Ginger Rice

Serves 4
Preparation 10mins
plus marinating
Cooking 25mins
Calories 362
Fat 1.3g

455g/1 lb skinless chicken breast or thigh fillets or tenderloin, trimmed of visible fat

Soy and Honey Marinade
1 tbsp sesame seeds, toasted
1 tbsp rice wine (mirin) or sherry
2 tsp honey or plum sauce
2 tsp reduced-salt soy sauce
2 tsp oyster sauce
1 tsp sesame oil

Ginger Rice
1 tbsp finely chopped fresh ginger
1 tsp sesame oil
1 cup short or medium grain rice, rinsed and drained
$1^2/_5$ cups ginger beer
1 tbsp diced pickled or preserved ginger
1 tbsp finely chopped spring onion, optional

1 To make the marinade, place the sesame seeds, wine, sauces and sesame oil in a non-reactive bowl. Mix to combine.
2 Cut the chicken into large pieces. Add to the marinade. Toss to coat. Cover. Marinate in the refrigerator for at least 1 hour.
3 To make the rice, place fresh ginger and sesame oil in a large saucepan over a low heat. Cook, stirring occasionally, for 5 minutes. Add the rice. Cook, stirring, for 2 minutes. Stir in the ginger beer and pickled ginger. Bring to the boil. Reduce the heat. Cover. Steam for 10–15 minutes or until the liquid is absorbed and the rice is cooked. Stir in spring onion.
4 Meanwhile, preheat the grill or barbecue to a medium heat. Drain the chicken. Cook under the grill or on the barbecue, brushing occasionally with marinade, for 6–7 minutes or until cooked through and slightly crispy on the outside. The chicken is cooked when the juices run clear when pressed with a fork. Serve chicken with the Ginger Rice and steamed Chinese greens.

Malaysian Grilled Chicken

4 skinless chicken breasts on the bone
2 tsp cornflour blended with 2 tbsp water
cucumber slices
red pepper strips, optional

Spicy Oriental Marinade
1 red onion, quartered
2 cloves garlic, chopped
1 tbsp grated fresh ginger
1 tbsp ground coriander
1 tbsp palm sugar, crumbled, or brown sugar
1 tsp Chinese five spice powder
$^1/_4$ cup rice wine (mirin)
$^1/_4$ cup orange or lime juice
1 tbsp reduced-salt thick dark soy sauce

1 To make the marinade, place the onion and garlic in a food processor. Process to finely chop. Transfer to a bowl. Add the ginger, coriander, sugar, five spice powder, wine, orange juice and soy sauce. Mix to combine.
2 Place the chicken in a shallow glass or ceramic dish. Pour over the marinade. Turn to coat. Cover. Marinate in the refrigerator overnight. Transfer the chicken and marinade to a large non-stick frying pan.
3 Place the pan over a medium heat. Bring to the boil. Reduce the heat. Simmer for 15–20 minutes or until chicken is just tender; take care not to overcook. Using a slotted spoon, remove the chicken from the cooking liquid. Place in a clean dish. Cover. Refrigerate until ready to barbecue or stir-fry. Reserve the marinade.
4 Preheat the barbecue to a medium heat. Cook the chicken on barbecue grill for 5 minutes each side or until

richly coloured and heated through. Alternatively, heat a little oil in a wok over a high heat. Add the chicken. Stir-fry for 3–4 minutes or until heated through.
5 Place the reserved marinade and the cornflour mixture in a small saucepan over a medium heat. Cook, stirring constantly, for 4–5 minutes or until the sauce boils and thickens.
6 To serve, spoon the sauce over the chicken and accompany with cucumber, red capsicum and steamed rice.

Serves 4
Preparation 8mins
plus marinating
Cooking 40mins
Calories 239
Fat 0.8g

Chicken Kebabs with Couscous

Serves 4
Preparation 30mins
+ 1 hour marinating
Cooking 12mins
Calories 499
Fat 14g

**4 chicken breast fillets (skin off)
cut into 24 pieces
1 yellow and 1 red capsicum,
deseeded and cut into 8 pieces
juice of 1 lemon
2 garlic cloves, crushed
2 tbsp extra virgin olive oil
1 tbsp chopped fresh coriander**

Sauce
**$3/5$ cup natural yoghurt
1 tbsp lemon juice
finely grated rind of $1/2$ lemon
sea salt and freshly ground
black pepper
4 large wooden skewers**

Couscous
**255g/9oz couscous
30g/1oz butter
4 spring onions, finely chopped
3 tbsp chopped fresh coriander**

1 Place the chicken and capsicums in a non-metallic bowl, add the lemon juice, garlic, olive oil and coriander and mix. Cover and leave to marinate for at least 1 hour. Meanwhile, combine all the ingredients for the sauce. Season with salt and pepper and leave to chill. Soak four large wooden skewers in water for about 10 minutes.

2 Preheat the grill to high. Thread the chicken and capsicums onto the skewers and grill for 10–12 minutes, turning occasionally, until the chicken is slightly charred, cooked through and tender. Keep warm.

3 Meanwhile, prepare the couscous according to packet instructions, then fluff up with a fork. Melt the butter in a small saucepan and fry the spring onions for about 2 minutes. Add the spring onions with 3 tablespoons of coriander and plenty of seasoning to the couscous and mix well. Serve the couscous on plates, with the kebabs on top, then drizzle with the yoghurt sauce.

Cajun Chicken Brochettes

3 large skinless boneless chicken
breasts, cut into 2¹/₂ cm/1in pieces
salt and black pepper
olive oil for brushing

Marinade
3 tbsp Dijon mustard
3 tbsp clear honey
1 tbsp olive oil
2 tbsp tomato sauce
¹/₂ tsp Tabasco
1 clove garlic, crushed
¹/₂ tsp dried thyme
3 basil leaves, finely chopped, plus
extra leaves to garnish
6 skewers

Peach Salsa
3 peaches, fresh or canned
85mL/3fl oz natural yoghurt
1 tsp lemon juice

1 To make the marinade, mix the
mustard, honey, oil, tomato sauce,
Tabasco, garlic, thyme and basil in a
shallow, non-metallic dish that is
large enough to hold 6 skewers.

If using wooden skewers, soak them
in water for 10 minutes.
2 Season the chicken, with a little
salt and pepper, then thread them
onto the skewers. Add to the
marinade and turn until coated. Cover
and place in the refrigerator for 1 hour,
stirring occasionally.
3 Meanwhile, make the peach salsa.
If using fresh peaches, put them into a
bowl, cover with boiling water and leave
for 30 seconds. Peel off the skins,
remove the stones and chop. If using
canned peaches, chop the flesh. Mix the
peaches with the yoghurt and lemon
juice, season with black pepper, cover
and refrigerate until needed.
4 Preheat the grill to high and brush
the rack with oil. Place the brochettes
on the grill rack, brush with half the
marinade and grill for 6 minutes.
Turn them over, brush with the rest
of the marinade and grill for a further
2–3 minutes, until the chicken is
tender and cooked through. Serve
with the salsa, garnished with basil.

*Note: Tender chunks
of chicken in a
piquant marinade
are set off by a peach
and yoghurt salsa.
You'll love it so
much you may want
to double the
quantities and serve
it as a main course.*

Serves 6
Preparation 25mins
+ 1 hr marinating
Cooking 10mins
Calories 181
Fat 6g

Chicken in a Salad

Diced, curried, tossed, coated, spiced and glazed - these lively salads are all dressed up and ready to party. Whether it's luncheon at the Waldorf, a big night at Caesar's or a romantic tropical getaway, all events are guaranteed to delight your guests. So get those lemons and limes away from the bar and into your kitchen. They've got a hot date with basil, Dijon, chilli, cayenne and paprika!

Chicken and Endive Salad with Creamy Dressing

OVEN TEMPERATURE
170°C, 335°F, GAS 3

Serves 4
Preparation 15mins
Cooking 4mins
Calories 355
Fat 3.1g

1 slender French bread stick (baguette)
1 clove garlic, crushed
2 tbsp oil
1 bunch curly endive, washed and drained dry
4 spring onions, sliced
225g/8oz can mandarin segments, drained (juice reserved)
225g/8oz chicken tenderloins

Dressing
1 cup coleslaw dressing
1 tsp Dijon mustard

1 Cut the bread stick into ¹/₂ cm/¹/₅ in slices. Mix the garlic and oil together and brush onto the bread slices. Place on a tray in a moderate oven and cook until crisp and golden. Break the endive into 5cm/2in pieces; mix with the spring onions and mandarin segments.
2 Cook the tenderloins in a lightly greased non-stick pan for 2 minutes each side.
3 Mound the croutons and endive salad onto individual serving plates and arrange the chicken on top. Mix the dressing ingredients together and pour on the top, allowing it to run down the sides. Serve as an entrée.

Chicken Waldorf

400g/14oz chicken breast fillets, poached
2 red apples
1 tbsp lemon juice
2 sticks celery, diced
55g/2oz blond walnuts, coarsely chopped
$^1/_2$ cup mayonnaise
1 lettuce, separated into cups, washed and crisped

1 Poach the chicken breasts (see tip), and cool. Cut into 1cm/$^1/_2$in cubes. Wash the apples well, leave the skin on and cut into 1cm/$^1/_2$in cubes. Sprinkle with the lemon juice.

2 Toss the chicken, apples, celery and walnuts together. Add the mayonnaise and gently toss through.

3 Spoon into the lettuce cups and serve as an entrée or light lunch, or line a salad bowl with lettuce leaves and pile the salad into the centre and serve for a buffet.

Tip: To poach the chicken: Cover the fillets with hot water, add a little salt, a small onion, chopped, a piece of celery and a carrot. Simmer for 20–25 minutes until tender. Remove the chicken to cool. Strain the stock, it can be reserved for future use. Discard the vegetables.

Serves 6   **Preparation** 10mins   **Cooking** 25mins   **Calories** 226   **Fat** 1.7g

Chicken Caesar Salad

Tip: To make croutons. Use unsliced day-old white bread. Cut slices 1¹/₂cm/¹/₂ in thick, remove crusts and cut into 1¹/₂cm/ ¹/₂ in cubes. Peel 2 cloves of garlic and cut them in half. Add enough oil to be 5mm/¹/₄ in deep in the frying pan, add the garlic and heat. Remove garlic when golden; add the bread cubes, stir and toss as they fry to golden colour. Remove quickly from the pan and drain on paper towels.

Tip: To joint a chicken. Remove the leg and thigh at the joint. Separate the leg and thigh cutting through the joint. Remove the wings at the joint. Cut the breast from the backbone along the fine rib bones on each side. Cut through the centre breast bone. Cut each breast into 2 pieces.

2 chicken breast fillets
1 clove garlic, crushed
salt and pepper
2 tsp olive oil
1 tbsp lemon juice
1 Romaine lettuce

Dressing
2 anchovy fillets
4 tbsp olive oil
2¹/₂ tbsp lemon juice
¹/₂ tsp salt
¹/₄ tsp pepper
1 coddled egg
pinch of dry mustard
1 tsp Worcestershire sauce
¹/₄ cup grated Parmesan cheese
1 cup garlic croutons
shaved Parmesan cheese for garnish

1 Trim the chicken fillets. Mix together the garlic, salt, pepper, oil and lemon juice, cover and marinate the chicken for 30 minutes in the refrigerator. Heat grill or chargrill until hot. Sear the fillets 1 minute on each side, then cook for 3 minutes each side. Remove and rest for 5 minutes before cutting into ¹/₂ cm/¹/₅ in slices on the diagonal.
2 Separate the leaves of the lettuce, discard outer leaves and wash well. Drain and shake dry in a clean tea towel. Cut the greener leaves into bite-sized pieces and leave the pale inner leaves whole. Cover and place in the refrigerator until ready for use.

3 Place the anchovy fillets in base of the salad bowl and mash with the back of a fork while the oil is being added. Gradually add the lemon juice while beating and sprinkle in the salt and pepper. Break in the coddled egg, scraping the set white from inside the shell and lightly stir. Add the mustard and Worcestershire sauce.
4 Add the lettuce leaves; toss to coat lightly with dressing while sprinkling over the grated Parmesan cheese. Toss in the chicken and croutons. Rearrange the whole leaves to stand upright and garnish with the shaved Parmesan cheese. Serve immediately.

To coddle an egg. Bring the egg to room temperature. Boil water in a small saucepan and when it reaches the boil, turn the heat off and immediately lower in the egg. Stand for 1 minute in the water. If the egg is cold from refrigerator, allow 1¹/₂ minutes.

Serves 5
Preparation 8mins plus marinating
Cooking 8mins plus 5mins resting
Calories 297
Fat 3.9g

Crunchy Chicken and Potato Salad

Serves 6
Preparation 10mins
Cooking 20mins plus
20mins potatoes
Calories 276
Fat 2.3g

455g/1 lb potatoes, medium-sized
water to cover
1 tsp salt
1 tbsp olive oil
1 large onion, finely chopped
1 clove garlic, crushed

200g/7oz minced chicken meat
1 tbsp lemon juice
salt and pepper to taste
1 cup mayonnaise
1 small red chilli, seeded and
finely chopped (optional)
dill feathers to garnish
small lettuce leaves to garnish

1 Wash and peel the potatoes and cut each into 4–6 wedges. Place in boiling water to cover, add salt and cook for 20 minutes. Drain and cool.

2 Heat the oil in a large frying pan, add the onion and garlic and fry until the onion is soft. Stir in the minced chicken and brown while stirring continuously. This will take about 15 minutes. Add the lemon juice and stir up the cooked pan juices. When the minced chicken is brown and crumbly, season with a little salt and pepper, remove from the heat and cool.

3 Mix the cooled potatoes and ²/₃ of the minced chicken and the mayonnaise together gently, tossing in the chilli. Pile into a clean salad bowl or platter and pile ing the remaining minced chicken in a pile on the top. Garnish with dill feathers and surround with small lettuce leaves if desired. Serve as a luncheon salad or buffet item.

Curried Chicken Salad

1 large, ready cooked barbecued
chicken
2 sticks celery, finely chopped
6 spring onions, sliced
$^1/_3$ cup raisins, soaked
55g/2oz slivered almonds, toasted
200g/7oz mixed salad greens,
washed and crisped
assorted fresh fruits to garnish
toasted shredded coconut
to garnish

Dressing
$^3/_5$ cup mayonnaise
$^3/_5$ cup low-fat yoghurt
3 tbsp sweet mango chutney
1 tbsp mild curry paste
2 tbsp lemon juice
2 tsp freshly grated
lemon zest

1 Remove the chicken meat from
the bones and cut into bite-size
pieces. Toss with the celery, spring
onions, raisins and almonds.
2 Place all dressing ingredients in a
bowl and whisk until smooth.
3 Pour the dressing over the
chicken and toss to mix through.
Cover and chill for 2 hours or
more. Line a platter or individual
plates with salad greens and pile on
the chicken mixture.
Garnish with fruits and coconut.

*Note: Quantities
given are for 8 rolls.
Make adjustments
for number required.
Other salad
vegetables and fruit
may be used
according to
preference, eg:
avocado, grated
carrot, celery,
pineapple, nuts, etc.*

Serves 8
Preparation 10mins
plus chilling
Cooking nil
Calories 500
Fat 4.7g

Warm Salad of Mustard-Glazed Chicken with Red Wine Vinaigrette

OVEN TEMPERATURE
210°C, 410°F, GAS 6

Serves 8
Preparation 10mins
plus marinating
Cooking 30mins
Calories 351
Fat 2.5g

3 tbsp mustard seeds
3 tbsp malt vinegar
2 tbsp honey
1 tbsp molasses
1 tbsp brown sugar
$^1/_2$ cup olive oil
4 tbsp French mustard
2 cloves garlic, minced
$^1/_2$ cup boiling water
8 skinless chicken breast fillets
2 tbsp red or white wine vinegar
2 tbsp olive oil
salt and pepper to taste
285g/10oz assorted baby lettuce
leaves, well washed and dried
285g/10oz baby spinach leaves,
well washed and dried
1 bunch spring onions, sliced on
the diagonal
1 bunch chives, chopped

1 To make the marinade, grind two tablespoons of the mustard seeds into powder, then mix with the malt vinegar, honey molasses, brown sugar, olive oil, French mustard, garlic and boiling water. Whisk well until the mixture is thick and smooth.

2 Reserve 4 tablespoons of marinade for later use. Lay the chicken in a flat glass dish and pour the remaining marinade over. Turn the chicken so that both sides are covered in the marinade and chill for at least 4 hours.

3 Remove the chicken from the marinade, making sure that each piece of chicken has a good coating of the marinade. Place in an ovenproof baking dish or on an oven tray and bake for 20–25 minutes, until cooked through.

4 Meanwhile, transfer the reserved marinade to a saucepan and bring to the boil. Simmer for 5 minutes then remove from the heat. Remove the chicken from the oven and keep warm.

5 Make a dressing with the red or white wine vinegar and olive oil with salt and pepper to taste and a little of the reserved warm marinade. Whisk well. Toss some dressing through the mixed lettuce and spinach leaves just to coat them. Add the spring onions and chives and toss again.

6 To serve, arrange the salad leaves on plates then top each mound of salad with a chicken breast, sliced on the diagonal. Drizzle around a little remaining warm marinade.

Party Avocado and Chicken Salad

Serves 10–20
Preparation 12mins
Cooking 25mins
Calories 147
Fat 1.9g

900g/2 lb chicken breast fillets
3 avocados
1 tbsp lemon juice
2 sticks celery, thinly sliced
55g/2oz slivered almonds, toasted
$1/_2$ green capsicum cut into slices
400g/14oz can mango slices,
drained
(or fresh mango in season)
1 cucumber
lettuce to serve

Dressing
1 cup thickened cream, whipped
$1/_2$ cup mayonnaise
$1/_2$ grated nutmeg
1 tsp paprika
salt and pepper

1 Poach the chicken as given on page 31, cool then cut into large dice $1^1/_2$ cm–$2^1/_2$ cm/$^1/_2$ in–1in cubes. Peel and slice the avocado and sprinkle with lemon juice.
2 Combine the chicken, celery, almonds, capsicum and most of the avocado, mango slices and cucumber.
3 Mix the dressing ingredients together, pour over the salad and toss gently. Arrange the lettuce leaves on a shallow platter; pile on the chicken mixture. Garnish with the reserved avocado, mango and cucumber.

Tossed Greens and Chicken with Blue Cheese Dressing

1 bunch rocket
1 coral lettuce
1 mignonette lettuce
1 red apple, cored, thinly sliced,
splashed with lemon juice
55g/2oz pale walnut pieces
2 poached chicken breasts
(see tip on Page 31)

Dressing
$^1/_3$ cup olive oil
2 tbsp white wine vinegar
1 tbsp lemon juice
$^1/_4$ tsp sugar
1 tbsp Dijon mustard
30g/1oz blue-vein cheese,
crumbled
pinch cayenne
55g/2oz extra blue-vein cheese
for topping

1 Wash the greens, drain and shake in a tea towel to dry. Arrange on 4 individual plates with apple slices and $^1/_2$ the pieces.
2 Cut the chicken into slices and arrange with the salad greens. Whisk the dressing ingredients together and pour over each salad. Sprinkle the top with remaining walnut pieces and extra crumbled blue-vein cheese. Serve as an entrée or luncheon dish.

Serves 4–5
Preparation 10mins
Cooking 25mins
Calories 318
Fat 3g

Tropical Chicken Salad

Serves 4
Preparation 10mins
Cooking 10mins plus refrigeration
Calories 321
Fat 1.7g

2 large skinless chicken breast fillets
1 Lebanese cucumber, diced
1 cup diced fresh or unsweetened canned pineapple
$^1/_2$ cup diced pawpaw
$^1/_4$ cup unsalted cashews
2 green onions, sliced diagonally
2 tbsp chopped fresh coriander
2 tbsp chopped fresh mint

Chilli and Lime Dressing
1 fresh red chilli, thinly sliced
finely grated zest of 1 lime
juice of 2 limes
1 tbsp fish sauce
1 tbsp rice wine vinegar
$^1/_2$ tsp sesame oil

1 Preheat the barbecue to a high heat.
2 Cook the chicken on the barbecue grill for 4–5 minutes each side or until cooked through. Alternatively, place the chicken in a frying pan and pour water or a mixture of water and wine to cover it. Cover. Bring to simmering. Poach for 10 minutes or until the chicken is cooked. Cool. Cut into thin strips.
3 Place the chicken, cucumber, pineapple, pawpaw, cashews, green onions, coriander and mint in a bowl. Toss to combine.
4 To make the dressing, place the chilli, lime zest and juice, fish sauce, vinegar and oil in a screwtop jar. Shake to combine. Drizzle the dressing over the salad. Toss. Cover. Refrigerate for at least 15 minutes before serving - this allows the flavours to develop.

Asian Chicken and Kaffir Lime Salad

2–3 (about 400g/14oz) skinless chicken breast fillets
4 kaffir lime leaves, finely shredded
1 lime, sliced
115g/4oz Chinese (mung bean) vermicelli
225g/8oz green beans, halved
1 cup fresh coriander leaves
1 cup fresh Thai basil leaves, shredded
4 spring onions, thinly sliced
2 tbsp fried shallots

Dressing
2 tbsp fish sauce
2 tbsp lime juice
2 tbsp palm sugar, grated

1 Put the chicken in a large, deep fry pan, add the kaffir lime leaves and lime slices and cover with water. Bring to the boil.

Reduce the heat to a very slow simmer and poach the chicken for 15 minutes or until tender. Drain the chicken, reserving 55mL/2fl oz of the liquid. Allow the chicken to cool slightly then shred finely using your fingers.

2 While the chicken is cooking, put the vermicelli in a bowl and cover with boiling water. Allow to stand for 5–10 minutes or until tender, then drain well. Cook the beans until tender then drain.

3 Put the chicken, vermicelli, coriander, basil, beans, spring onions and shallots into a bowl and toss to combine.

4 To make the dressing, put the reserved cooking liquid, fish sauce, lime juice and palm sugar in a jug and whisk well. Pour over the salad and toss to combine.

Serves 4
Preparation 20mins
Cooking 15mins
Calories 209
Fat 3.1g

Chicken in a Pan

If you ever doubted that chicken goes with everything, the proof is about to appear in your saucepan. Chicken and shiitake? 'Hai!' Chicken and prosciutto? 'Si!' Chicken and Redang?' 'Ya!' Chicken and banana? 'No worries, Mate!' From Japan to Italy and Indonesia to Australia, chicken speaks everyone's language and is at home in all cultures. So go ahead, think globally and cook locally!

Tandoori Chicken Pockets

*Note: For extra
flavour, serve with a
spoonful of your
favourite chutney.*

Makes 12
Preparation 10mins
Cooking 15mins
Calories 132
Fat 0.7g

2 tsp canola oil
1 small onion, finely chopped
900g/2 lb chicken stirfry,
chopped to smaller pieces
$^1\!/_2$ tsp salt
2 tsp tandoori curry paste
1 tbsp lemon juice
1 tbsp water
1 packet white
or wholemeal pita bread pockets
3 cups shredded lettuce
$2^1\!/_2$ cups natural yoghurt

1 Heat the oil in a small pan, add the onion and fry until soft. Sprinkle the chicken with salt and fry until almost cooked. Stir in the curry paste, cook a little, then add the lemon juice and water. Allow to simmer until most of the liquid has evaporated. Stir occasionally.

2 Cut pita bread in half and open the pocket. Place the lettuce in the base of the pocket and fill with the curried chicken. Add a tablespoon of yoghurt on top. Serve immediately.

Chicken Breasts with Shiitake Mushrooms

2 tbsp groundnut oil
1 onion, chopped
5cm/2in piece fresh root ginger,
finely chopped
200g/7oz shiitake mushrooms,
stems removed and caps sliced
145g/5oz baby button
mushrooms
2 tbsp dark soy sauce
1 cup chicken stock
1 cup white wine
340g/12oz patty pan squash,
halved, or zucchini,
trimmed and sliced
6 skinless boneless chicken
breasts
chopped fresh coriander
to garnish

1 Preheat the oven. Heat
1 tablespoon of the oil in a large,
heavy-based saucepan, add the
onion and the ginger and fry for
5 minutes or until the onion has
softened. Add the shiitake and
button mushrooms and the soy
sauce and cook for a further
4–5 minutes, until the mushrooms
have softened.

Serves 6
Preparation 15mins
Cooking 50mins
Calories 278
Fat 11g

2 Stir in the stock and wine,
bring to the boil, then simmer for
10 minutes. Add the squash or
zucchini and cook for a further 5
minutes or until tender.
3 Meanwhile, make 3 slashes in
each chicken breast, using a sharp
knife. Heat the remaining oil in a
large, heavy-based frying pan, add
the chicken and fry for 2–3
minutes each side to brown.
4 Transfer the chicken to an
ovenproof dish and spoon over the
mushroom mixture. Bake for
15–20 minutes, until the chicken is
cooked through. Sprinkle with
coriander just before serving.

OVEN TEMPERATURE
230°C, 450°F, GAS 8

Note: Shiitake
mushrooms, soy
sauce and fresh
ginger give this dish
an oriental flavour.
It's great with plain
boiled rice or
Chinese noodles and
some stir-fried green
vegetables.

Italian Chicken in a Pan

Serves 6
Preparation 10mins
plus refrigeration
Cooking 15mins
Calories 412
Fat 3.2g

6 boneless, skinless
chicken breast fillets
seasoned flour
1 egg, beaten
dried breadcrumbs
$\frac{1}{4}$ cup vegetable oil
2 cups bottled tomato pasta sauce
6 slices prosciutto or ham
6 slices mozzarella cheese
6 sprigs fresh sage

1 Place the chicken between sheets of greaseproof paper and pound lightly to flatten. Dust with the flour, then dip in the egg and finally coat with the breadcrumbs. Place on a plate lined with plastic food wrap and refrigerate for 15 minutes.

2 Heat the oil in a large frying pan over a medium heat, add the chicken and cook for 2–3 minutes each side or until golden. Remove from the pan and set aside.

3 Add the pasta sauce to the pan and cook over a medium heat, stirring, for 4–5 minutes or until hot. Place the chicken in a single layer on top of the sauce, then top each fillet with a slice of prosciutto or ham, a slice of cheese and a sprig of sage. Cover and simmer for 5 minutes or until the chicken is cooked through and the cheese melts. Serve immediately.

Marinated Chicken Salad

2 cups vegetable oil
455g/1 lb chicken stirfry
$^1/_2$ cup seasoned flour
$^1/_4$ cup orange juice
$^1/_4$ cup olive oil
1 tbsp mint, chopped
$^1/_2$ tsp salt
freshly ground black pepper
1 avocado, sliced
400g/14oz can apricot halves
1 punnet snow pea sprouts

1 Heat the oil in a deep frying pan. Dip the stirfry strips in the flour, a few at a time, and deep-fry in the hot oil until cooked and golden in colour. Drain on absorbent paper, then place in a glass bowl.

2 Combine the orange juice, oil, mint, salt and pepper in a screw-top jar and shake well. Pour over the chicken strips and refrigerate for at least 30 minutes.

3 Slice the avocado and drain the apricot halves, reserving two tablespoons of juice from the can. Arrange the snow pea sprouts on individual plates. Top with the chicken strips, avocado pieces and apricot halves. Add 1–2 teaspoons of juice to the remaining marinade and drizzle over the salad. Serve as an entrée or as a luncheon dish with crusty bread.

Serves 6-8
Preparation 10mins
plus refrigertion
Cooking 10mins
Calories 229
Fat 1.8g

Orange and Spice Leg Steaks

Tip: To debone drumsticks. With a sharp-pointed knife, cut around the knuckle at the top of the legs then holding onto the knob, scrape meat around the bone to detach the meat. Pull the bone out. If this is too difficult, slit through to the bone down the length, then cut the bone out. Fold back into original shape.

Serves 3-4
Preparation 30mins plus standing
Cooking 17mins
Calories 271
Fat 3.2g

455g/1 lb (6) chicken drumsticks
1 tsp minced ginger
$^1/_2$ tsp ground nutmeg
$^1/_2$ tsp ground cinnamon
2 tbsp canola oil
2 large oranges
1 tsp brown sugar
watercress to garnish

1 Remove the bone and skin from each drumstick (see tip). With a sharp knife, make 3 diagonal slashes on both sides to cut through the smooth covering membrane. Place each drumstick between 2 sheets of plastic wrap and pound each side with a meat mallet to thin out. It may be necessary to snip through more membrane as you pound.

2 Mix the ginger, nutmeg and cinnamon together. Rub the spices all over the chicken, including the slashes and the centre from where the bone was removed. Stand for at least 30 minutes for flavour to penetrate.
3 Heat the oil until hot, in a large non-stick frying pan. Add the chicken and sear quickly for 1 minute each side. Turn the heat down to medium and fry the chicken for 4 minutes each side.
Remove to a plate. Pour off most of the oil from the pan. Thinly peel the zest off 1 orange with a potato peeler and cut into julienne strips or remove the zest with a zester. Juice the oranges.
4 Stir the orange juice into the pan, place over a low heat, scrape up and dissolve any cooked-on juices. Stir in the brown sugar and zest. Bring to a steady simmer while stirring.
5 Return the chicken to the pan, quickly turn to coat and glaze with sauce as it thickens, taking care not to evaporate sauce too much.
6 Transfer chicken to a serving plate and spoon over the sauce. Pile the zest on top. Garnish with an orange slice and a sprig of watercress. Serve with rice or mashed potato.

Tangy Tenderloins

455g/1 lb chicken tenderloins
salt and pepper
olive oil spray
200g/7oz sugar peas
400g/14oz can baby corn,
drained
$^1/_2$ cup apricot nectar
2 tbsp cider vinegar
2 tbsp sweet chilli sauce

1 Flatten the tenderloins slightly and sprinkle with salt and pepper. Heat a heavy-based frying pan and spray lightly with oil spray. Add the tenderloins and cook for 2 minutes each side. Remove from the pan.
2 Add the sugar peas and stir around the pan until they brighten in colour. Add the corn.
Return the chicken to the pan and toss with the vegetables. Combine the 2 sauces and vinegar. Pour over the chicken and vegetables and heat through. Pile onto serving plates. Serve immediately.

Serves 5
Preparation 8mins
Cooking 10mins
Calories 207
Fat 0.5g

Risotto of Indian Spiced Chicken with Chickpeas

Note: The aromatic spices that marinate the chicken create delicious musky flavours that permeate the rice. The chicken will benefit from a marination of at least 6 hours, but if time is scarce, at 1–2 hours will do.

Serves 6
Preparation 10mins
plus marinating
Cooking 20mins
Calories 638
Fat 2.7g

3 cloves garlic, crushed
2 tsp ground cumin
2 tsp paprika
2 tsp ground coriander
1 tbsp Garam Masala
1 tsp ground ginger
3 tbsp mango or apricot chutney
juice and zest of 1 orange
4 tbsp olive oil
4 boneless, skinless thigh fillets cut into strips, or 12 'winglets'
1 tbsp ghee
1 bunch spring onions, trimmed and chopped
400g/14oz arborio rice
4 cups well flavoured vegetable stock
400g/14oz can chickpeas, drained and rinsed
2 handfuls baby spinach, washed
115g/4oz sultanas
2 tbsp yoghurt, optional
2 tbsp fresh mint, chopped
salt and freshly ground black pepper
115g/4oz toasted almonds

1 In a glass jug, mix together the garlic, cumin, paprika, coriander, Garam Marsala, ginger, chutney, orange juice and zest and oil. Mix very well then pour over the chicken in a non-reactive baking dish (glass or ceramic) and allow to marinate for 6 hours overnight.

2 In a saucepan, heat the ghee and add $1/2$ the spring onions and cook gently until softened. Remove the chicken from the marinade and add to the spring onions, cooking until the chicken begins to change colour, about 3 minutes.

3 Remove the chicken from the pan, add the rice and begin adding the stock, half a cup at a time and allowing each to be absorbed before the next quantity of stock is added. When adding the last of the stock, add the chickpeas, baby spinach and sultanas and mix vigorously to incorporate. When the liquid has been absorbed, remove the saucepan from the heat and add the remaining spring onions, yoghurt, fresh mint and salt and pepper to taste.
Serve immediatley, garnished with the almonds.

Chicken Rolls with an Indonesian Flavour

Serves 4
Preparation 15mins
Cooking 40mins
Calories 493
Fat 10.1g

900g/2 lb chicken thigh fillets
285g/10oz Redang curry sauce
2 bananas
toothpicks
2 tbsp vegetable oil
$^1/_2$ cup water
$^3/_5$ cup coconut milk
1 small, fresh pineapple,
peeled, and thinly sliced
freshly ground black pepper
2 tbsp shredded coconut, toasted
steamed rice to serve

1 Open out the fillets on a large chopping board. Flatten with a meat mallet to an even thinness. Spread each with a teaspoon of Rendang curry sauce.
2 Peel the bananas and slit them in half lengthwise then cut them in half to make 4 pieces. Place a piece of banana in centre of each fillet and form into a roll. Fasten with a toothpick. Heat the oil in a wide-based saucepan and brown the rolls on all sides, a few at a time, removing them to a plate as they brown. Drain all the oil from the saucepan.
3 To the same saucepan, add the Rendang curry sauce and the water. Bring to the boil, reduce the heat to a simmer and place in the chicken rolls. Cover and simmer 35 minutes, turning the rolls once during cooking.
4 Remove the rolls to a heated platter and keep hot. If the sauce is thin, increase the heat and reduce the sauce to a thicker consistency. Reduce the heat and stir in the coconut milk and simmer for 2 minutes. Return the rolls to the saucepan to reheat.
5 Saute the pineapple rings in a little butter until lightly coloured and grind over some black pepper. Arrange 1–2 slices of pineapple and a chicken roll on each plate, spoon the sauce over the roll and sprinkle with a little toasted coconut. Serve with steamed rice.

Chicken Wings Moroccan Style

2 tbsp canola oil
900g/2 lb chicken wings
1 large onion, finely chopped
1 clove garlic, crushed
1¹/₂ tsp chopped fresh ginger
¹/₂ tsp ground turmeric
¹/₂ tsp cumin
¹/₂ cinnamon stick
¹/₄ cup cider vinegar
425mL/15fl oz apricot nectar
salt and pepper
85g/3oz dried prunes, pitted
85g/3oz dried apricots
1 tbsp honey
¹/₄ cup lemon juice
steamed couscous or rice to serve

1 Heat the oil in a wide-based saucepan or lidded skillet. Add the chicken wings, a few at a time, and brown lightly on both sides. Remove to a plate as they brown.

2 Add the onion and fry for 2 minutes. Stir in the garlic, ginger and spices, cook while stirring for 1 minute, return the chicken to the pan, stir and turn the wings to coat with spices. Add the vinegar and apricot nectar and season to taste. Cover and simmer for 25 minutes.

3 Add the prunes, apricots, honey and lemon juice. Cover and simmer for 10 minutes and then remove lid and simmer uncovered for 5 minutes.
If a thicker sauce is desired, remove the wings and fruit to a serving platter, increase the heat and boil until the sauce reduces and thickens, stirring occasionally. Pour the sauce over the wings. Serve immediately with steamed couscous or rice.

Serves 3-4
Preparation 8mins
Cooking 50mins
Calories 628
Fat 2.6g

Hawaiian Poached Chicken

Serves 6
Preparation 10mins
Cooking 40–45mins
Calories 443
Fat 2.1g

$1^1/_3$ kg/3 lb fresh chicken
$^1/_2$ tsp each salt and pepper
1 tsp paprika
2 tbsp oil
1 large onion, chopped
1 clove garlic, crushed
$^1/_4$ cup water
1 tbsp Worcestershire sauce
2 tsp sweet chilli sauce
$^1/_4$ cup apple cider vinegar
$1^1/_2$ tbsp brown sugar
$^1/_2$ medium, fresh pineapple, peeled and diced
1 green capsicum, seeded and cut into thin strips
1 red capsicum, seeded and cut into thin strips
1 tbsp rum (optional)
$1^1/_2$ tbsp cornflour
$1^1/_2$ tbsp water
boiled rice to serve

1 Joint the chicken into serving pieces per the tip on page 32. Season with salt, pepper and paprika. Heat the oil in a large saucepan. Add the chicken pieces, a few at a time, and brown on all sides. Remove to a plate lined with kitchen paper as they brown.
2 Add the onion and garlic to the saucepan and cook, stirring for 2 minutes. Return the chicken to the saucepan. Combine the water, the 2 sauces, the vinegar and the sugar and pour over the chicken. Add the pineapple and capsicums. Simmer for 25–30 minutes until chicken is tender.
3 Warm and flame the rum and pour into the chicken. Blend the cornflour and water together, add to the chicken and stir through. Allow to simmer until it thickens. Increase the heat until it boils then turn off immediately. Serve with boiled rice.

Poached Chicken with Tomato and Mushroom Sauce

I medium-sized onion, finely chopped
1 clove garlic, finely chopped
3 large, ripe tomatoes, blanched, peeled and chopped or
1 can peeled whole tomatoes)
85g/3oz mushrooms, sliced
1 tbsp chopped fresh basil
$^3/_4$ cup water
1 tsp dried oregano
freshly ground black pepper
2 chicken breast fillets (skin off)
1 cup pasta twists
$^1/_2$ tsp olive oil
grated Parmesan cheese to serve (optional)

1 Place the onion, garlic, tomatoes and mushrooms in a wide-based saucepan over a moderate heat. Stir until they begin to soften. Add the basil, water, oregano and pepper, heat a little and add the chicken. Cover and simmer slowly for 20 minutes until chicken is tender. Do not allow to boil.

2 In another saucepan, cook the pasta twists in boiling water for 16–18 minutes. Drain and stir through the olive oil.

3 When the chicken is cooked, remove to a plate. If sauce is too thin, turn up the heat and boil until it reduces and thickens. Pour over the chicken and serve with pasta twists. Sprinkle with Parmesan cheese.

Serves 2–3
Preparation 8mins
Cooking 25mins
Calories 320
Fat 1g

Australian-Style Chicken Curry

Serves 2–3
Preparation 10mins
Cooking 55mins
Calories 456
Fat 1.8g

455g/1 lb chicken thigh fillets
2 tbsp oil
1 large onion, finely chopped
255g/9oz can Madras curry
cooking sauce
2 tbsp sultanas
2 bananas, sliced
1 green apple, peeled,
cored and cut into large dice
boiled rice to serve

1 Cut the chicken thighs into 2–3 pieces. Heat ¹/₂ the oil in a large saucepan, add ¹/₃ of the chicken and quickly brown on both sides. Remove to a plate and brown the remaining chicken in 2 batches, adding the remaining oil as necessary. Remove the last batch of chicken.

2 Add the onion and cook a little then stir in the Madras curry cooking sauce. Add a little water to the can to rinse down the remaining sauce (about a ¹/₄ can) and pour into the saucepan. Bring to the boil, turn down the heat and return the chicken to the saucepan. Cover and simmer for 20 minutes. Add the sultanas, banana and apple and simmer for 15–20 minutes more. Serve immediately with boiled rice.

Chicken Minestrone

olive oil spray
1 onion, finely chopped
1 clove garlic, chopped
1 stick celery, diced
1 carrot, peeled and diced
400g/14oz can peeled tomatoes
(no added salt)
4 cups water
freshly ground black pepper
1 tsp dried oregano
1 tsp mixed spice
2 tbsp chopped parsley
$^1/_2$ cup cut macaroni
$^1/_4$ cabbage, shredded
1 cup frozen baby peas
200g/7oz chicken stirfry or
chicken breast, chopped
crusty bread to serve

1 Lightly spray the base of a large saucepan with olive oil spray. Add the onion and garlic, stirring over the heat until they colour a little. Add the celery and carrot and continue to stir over the heat for 1 minute.

2 Chop the tomatoes and add to the saucepan with the juice. Stir in the water, pepper, oregano, spice and parsley. Bring to the boil and add the macaroni, stir until the soup returns to the boil, turn down to a simmer and cook for 15 minutes.

3 Stir in the cabbage, peas and chicken stirfry. Simmer for 15–20 minutes. Serve hot with crusty bread.

Tip: Left-over soup can be frozen for later use.

Serves 4–6
Preparation 15mins
Cooking 40mins
Calories 117
Fat 0.2g

Chicken in an Oven

Wings, schnitzels, drumsticks, nuggets, loaves and lasagna. This red hot section contains all your favorite recipes, plus a few new ones to increase your repertoire. Here you'll learn to make the most of every part of the marvelous chicken. In no time you'll be heading to the market with new confidence and a fresh sense of purpose. Load up your oven with these masterpieces and we guarantee you'll be counting the minutes until its time to taste success.

Apricot Glazed Chicken with Savoury Stuffing

OVEN TEMPERATURE
180°C, 350°F, GAS 4

Tip: To test for doneness, pierce the thickest part of breast and thigh with a skewer. If the juices run clear, the chicken is cooked. If the juices have a pink tinge, more cooking is needed.

Serves 4
Preparation 15mins
Cooking 90mins plus gravy
Calories 782
Fat 3.4g

1¹/₃ kg/3 lb fresh chicken
1 tbsp soy sauce
¹/₂ lemon

Apricot Dipping Sauce
¹/₂ cup apricot jam
1 tbsp soy sauce
1 tbsp lemon juice
2 tbsp white vinegar
1 tbsp water

Easy Stuffing
3–4 rashers bacon, chopped
1 large onion, finely chopped
1¹/₂ cups long-grain rice, rinsed
3 cups boiling water
2 tsp soy sauce
2 tsp mixed dried herbs
2 tbsp chopped parsley
1 tbsp flour, for gravy

1 To make the sauce, mix all the sauce ingredients together and heat gently while stirring.

2 Prepare the chicken for roasting. Mix together the Apricot Dipping Sauce and soy sauce, brush over the chicken and inside the cavity. Place the lemon half in the cavity. Place the chicken on an adjustable rack, breast-side down. Add a cup of water to the dish and cook in a preheated oven for 40 minutes. Brush again with sauce and turn breast-side up, brush with sauce and cook for 40–50 minutes more, until cooked when tested.

3 When the chicken is placed in the oven, prepare the stuffing. Place all ingredients in a lidded casserole dish and place on a shelf in the oven under the chicken. Cook for 40 minutes then remove from oven and stand covered for 10 minutes. When the chicken is cooked, remove from the dish and cover with foil to rest. Skim the fat from roasting the pan and add about 1 cup of water to dissolve any cooked-on pan juices. Pour into a small saucepan. Add 1 tablespoon of flour blended with a little water and stir until it thickens and boils.

4 Carve the chicken and serve with the stuffing, gravy and vegetable accompaniments.

Crunchy Drumsticks

OVEN TEMPERATURE
180°C, 350°F, GAS 4

Tip: A shallow dish is recommended as it aids the crisping process.

900g/2 lb chicken drumsticks
2 tbsp curry paste
2 cups vinegar-flavoured corn chips
or potato chips
boiled rice or salad
mild chutney for serving

1 Rinse the drumsticks and pat dry. With your fingers, rub the curry paste well into the skin of the drumsticks.

2 Crush the corn chips or potato chips and press onto the drumsticks. Place the drumsticks on a rack over a shallow baking tray. Bake in a preheated oven for 35–40 minutes.

3 Serve hot with boiled rice and some chutney on the side. May also be served cold with salad.

Serves 4   **Preparation** 10mins   **Cooking** 40mins   **Calories** 599   **Fat** 7.4g

Easy Apricot and Mango Chicken Loaf

700g/23oz minced chicken meat
55g/2oz fresh breadcrumbs
85g/3 oz spring onions, chopped
(including green part)
1 tbsp finely
chopped parsley
2 tbsp dried apricots
1 tbsp mango chutney
1 egg
1 tsp salt
$^1/_4$ tsp pepper
oil for greasing

1 Place the minced chicken in a large bowl. Add all remaining ingredients. With your hand, mix and knead the mixture for 2–3 minutes to combine ingredients well and to give a fine texture.
2 Grease a 22cm x 8cm x 5cm/ 9in x 3in x 2in loaf tin with oil. Pour in the mixture. Place in a preheated oven for 50–55 minutes. Test as per tip on Page 60. Rest in tin for 10 minutes before serving.
3 Serve hot with vegetable accompaniments or cold with salad.

OVEN TEMPERATURE
180°C, 350°F, GAS 4

Serves 6
Preparation 8mins
Cooking 55mins
Calories 329
Fat 1.4g

Oven Baked Chicken Schnitzels

OVEN TEMPERATURE
180°C, 350°F, GAS 4

Serves 5–6
Preparation 15mins
plus refrigeration
Cooking 16mins
Calories 349
Fat 1.4g

900g/2 lb chicken breast fillets
(skin off)
salt and pepper
juice of 1 lemon
2 tbsp sweet chilli sauce
$^3/_4$ cup flour
2 eggs
$1^1/_2$ cups dried breadcrumbs
olive oil spray

1 Place each fillet between 2 pieces of plastic wrap and flatten to an even thinness with the side of a meat mallet or rolling pin. Place on a platter. Mix the salt, pepper, lemon juice and chilli sauce together and pour over the chicken. Cover and refrigerate for 20 minutes.

2 Spread the flour onto a sheet of kitchen paper. Beat the eggs with one tablespoon of water and place in a shallow tray or dish. Spread the breadcrumbs onto a sheet of kitchen paper. Coat each side of the chicken fillets in flour (shake off excess) then egg and press into the breadcrumbs to coat both sides. Place on a flat surface in a single layer. Lightly spray the schnitzels with oil spray.
3 Place them oiled side down on a rack over an oven tray (a cake-rack is suitable). Lightly spray the top-side with oil spray. Place in a preheated oven and cook for 8 minutes, turn with tongs and cook for 8 minutes more.
4 Serve with vegetable accompaniments or a salad.

Quick Chicken Lasagne

455g/1 lb chicken thigh fillets
salt and pepper
1¹/₂ cups Paul Newman's Own
Tomato and Pesto Sauce (or
packaged sauce of choice)
225g/8oz instant lasagne sheets
85g/3oz mushrooms, sliced

Topping
225g/8oz ricotta cheese
200mL/7fl oz plain yoghurt
2 tbsp grated Romano
or Parmesan cheese
pinch nutmeg
2 eggs, lightly beaten

1 Place the fillets between 2 pieces of plastic wrap and pound with a meat mallet until thin. Season with salt and pepper.

2 Grease a baking dish or lasagne dish with oil. Spread a thin layer of sauce in the base of the dish. Dip 3–4 lasagne sheets into a dish of water and place to cover base. Spread them generously with sauce. Place the thigh fillets over the sauce in a single layer and cover with mushrooms. Wet 4 lasagne sheets and layer over the mushrooms. Spread the remaining sauce over the lasagne sheets.
3 Mix together all the topping ingredients and spread over the lasagne. Grate a little extra Parmesan over the surface and dot with small flecks of butter. Place in preheated oven for 35–40 minutes.
4 Stand for 10 minutes before serving for the lasagne sheets to re-absorb loose moisture.

OVEN TEMPERATURE
180°C, 350°F, GAS 4

Serves 6
Preparation 20mins
Cooking 40mins
Calories 382
Fat 4.5g

Satay Wings for a Crowd

Oven temperature
180°C, 350°F, Gas 4

Makes 32
Preparation 8mins
plus marinating
Cooking 40mins plus
5mins for sauce
Calories 80
Fat 0.9g

900g/2 lb chicken wings
3/4 cup Spicy Satay Sauce

Spicy Satay Sauce
3/4 cup peanut butter
3/4 cup water
2 tbsp brown sugar
1/8 tsp chilli powder, or to taste
1 tbsp soy sauce
1 tbsp grated onion
2 tbsp toasted sesame seeds
bamboo skewers, soaked

1 Rinse the wings and pat dry with a paper towel. Cut off each wing tip and discard. Cut through the next joint to make two pieces. Place all the wings in a bowl and stir through the satay sauce. Cover and marinate for 2 hours or more in the refrigerator; may be left overnight.

2 Arrange the wing pieces underside upward on a rack over a shallow dish or tray lined with foil. Place in a preheated oven for 15 minutes. Brush some of the remaining marinade on wing pieces, then turn them over and brush again. Cook for 20 minutes more. Brush with marinade, increase the heat to 200°C/400°F/Gas 5 and cook for about 5 minutes more.
3 Remove from the oven. Brush with 1 tablespoon of fresh satay sauce (do not use remaining marinade), to intensify the flavour.
4 Arrange on platter and serve hot as finger food.
5 To make the sauce, mix all ingredients in a saucepan, heat to a simmer. Keep on the heat for 5 minutes and allow to cool.

Tandoori Chicken

2 x 900g/2 lb fresh chickens
3 tbsp tandoori curry paste
200g/7oz tub natural yoghurt
2 tbsp lemon juice
2 tbsp melted butter
lettuce, onion rings, tomato
and lemon for serving

1 Rinse chickens inside and out and pat dry with paper towels. Make deep gashes in the thighs and on each side of breast. Pin back the wings.
2 Mix the tandoori paste, yoghurt, lemon juice and melted butter together. Place the chickens in a stainless steel or other non-metal dish and spread the mixture all over, rubbing well into the gashes. Cover and refrigerate for 12 or more hours. Place chickens on a roasting rack in a baking dish and spoon any remaining marinade over chickens.
3 Place in a preheated oven and cook for 1 hour. Baste with the pan juices during cooking.
When cooked cover with foil and rest for 10 minutes before serving. Arrange crisp lettuce leaves on a large platter and cover with onion rings. Cut chicken into portions and place on the platter. Garnish with tomato wedges and lemon slices.

OVEN TEMPERATURE
190°C, 370°F, GAS 5

Serves 8–10
Preparation 10mins
plus marinating
Cooking 1hr plus
10mins resting
Calories 235
Fat 2.1g

Roast Chicken with Basil and Red Onion

OVEN TEMPERATURE
190°C, 375°F, GAS 5

Note: Tucking basil leaves under the skin adds great flavour. The red onions are the perfect accompaniment.

1¹/₃ kg/3 lb chicken
15g/¹/₂ oz fresh basil
6 tbsp extra virgin olive oil
juice of ¹/₂ lemon
sea salt and freshly ground
black pepper

Onions
4 medium red onions
grated zest of ¹/₂ lemon
1 garlic clove, crushed

1 Preheat the oven. Place the chicken in a roasting tray. Gently work the skin away from the flesh with your fingers and tuck 6–7 basil leaves under the breast skin of the chicken. Place the remaining basil in a liquidiser with the olive oil, lemon juice and seasoning and blend until smooth. Brush the chicken with half the basil oil and cook for 40 minutes.

2 Meanwhile, prepare the onions. Peel them and slice off the root bottom to give a flat base. Make 4 cuts, in a criss-cross shape, across the top of each onion, coming only halfway down, so the onions open slightly. Combine the lemon zest with the garlic and sprinkle this over the onions.

3 Add the onions to the chicken in the tray and brush well with some of the basil oil. Brush the remaining oil over the chicken and cook for a further 40 minutes or until cooked through. Cover and allow the chicken to rest for 10 minutes before carving.

Serves 4
Preparation 20mins
+ 10mins resting
Cooking 1hr 10mins
Calories 502
Fat 35g

Oven-Baked Parmesan Chicken

**30g/1oz fresh breadcrumbs, made
from 1 slice stonebaked white
loaf, crusts removed
85g/3oz Parmesan, finely grated
2 spring onions, finely chopped
finely grated zest and juice of
¹/₂ lemon
55g/2oz butter, melted
sea salt and freshly ground
black pepper
4 skinless chicken breast fillets
2 tbsp chopped fresh parsley**

Serves 4
Preparation 25mins
Cooking 20mins
Calories 334
Fat 18g

1 Preheat the oven. Mix the breadcrumbs, Parmesan, spring onions, lemon zest, butter and seasoning together in a small bowl. Divide the mixture between the chicken breasts and, using a fork, press the mixture down on top, to form an even coat.

2 Transfer the chicken breasts to a shallow roasting tin and bake for 20 minutes. Remove the chicken from the roasting tin and keep warm. Add the lemon juice and parsley to the buttery juices in the tin and mix well. Pour these juices over the chicken and serve straight away.

OVEN TEMPERATURE
190°C, 375°F, GAS 5

*Note: Cooked in a coat of Parmesan and breadcrumbs, the chicken breasts keep moist and succulent.
Serve with new potatoes and a green vegetable or salad.*

Roasted Herby Chicken with Pears

OVEN TEMPERATURE
200°C, 400°F, GAS 6

Note: Sweet pears, chicken and fragrant herbs are a magical combination. The tarragon and rosemary add their flavour without overpowering the chicken.

juice of 2 lemons
salt and black pepper
12 chicken drumsticks, skinned
6 firm pears, peeled, halved, cored and cut crossways into 1cm/^{1}/$_2$ in slices
^{3}/$_5$ cup white wine
1 tbsp chopped fresh thyme or 1 tsp dried thyme
1 tbsp chopped fresh tarragon
1 tbsp chopped fresh rosemary

1 Mix together the lemon juice and seasoning. Put the drumsticks into a shallow, non-metallic bowl, pour over the seasoned lemon juice and rub into the skin with your fingertips. Cover and marinate in the fridge for 30 minutes.

2 Meanwhile, preheat the oven. Arrange the pears in a deep ovenproof dish, then top with the chicken and pour over the marinating juices. Pour over the wine and sprinkle with the thyme, tarragon and rosemary. Cover the dish with foil.

3 Cook for 1 hour, basting 1–2 times, until the chicken is tender. Remove the foil and increase the oven temperature to 230ºC/450ºF/Gas 8. Cook for a further 10 minutes or until the chicken is cooked through and the skin has browned. Leave it to rest, covered, for 10 minutes before serving.

Serves 6 **Preparation** 15mins 30mins marinating 10mins resting
Cooking 1hr 10mins **Calories** 374 **Fat** 25g

Asian Marinated Chicken Drumsticks

12 large chicken drumsticks
¹/₂ cup hoisin sauce
3 tbsp corn syrup
1 tbsp lemon juice
1 tbsp sunflower oil
2 cloves garlic, crushed
4 spring onions, thinly sliced on the diagonal
4 baby bok choy, halved
steamed rice, to serve

1 Remove the skin from the drumsticks and discard any excess fat. Make 2–3 deep slashes in the fleshy part of the chicken.

2 Put the sauce, corn syrup, lemon juice, oil and garlic in a large bowl and mix to combine. Coat the drumsticks with the mixture, cover and marinate in the refrigerator for 1 hour or overnight if you have time.

3 Preheat the oven. Line a baking tray with non stick paper. Put the drumsticks on the paper and roast for 40 minutes or until the juices run clear when tested with a skewer. Sprinkle the drumsticks with the spring onions.

4 Steam the bok choy in a bamboo steamer over a wok of simmering water, making sure the base of the steamer does not touch the water. Serve the chicken on top of the steamed bok choy with steamed rice on the side.

OVEN TEMPERATURE
200°C, 400°F, GAS 6

Serves 4
Preparation 20mins +
marinating
Cooking 40mins
Calories 325
Fat 8.6g

Roasted Herb Stuffed Chicken

OVEN TEMPERATURE
180°C, 350°F, GAS 4

Note: All the herbs need to be very finely chopped.

Serves 4-6
Preparation 12mins plus refrigeration
Cooking 17mins
Calories 263
Fat 4.1g

4 chicken breasts, skin on
2 tbsp thick natural yoghurt
1 clove garlic, crushed
1 tsp olive oil
2 tbsp mint, finely chopped
2 tbsp Italian parsley, finely chopped
2 tbsp oregano, finely chopped
2 tbsp thyme, finely chopped
2 tbsp fennel, finely chopped
2 spring onions, finely chopped
salt and finely ground black pepper

1 In a small bowl combine all ingredients except the chicken and mix well.
2 Using your fingertips, scoop up $1/4$ of the mixture and gently push it under the skin of the chicken. Run your fingers over the skin to smooth the stuffing out. Repeat with the remaining pieces. Cover and refrigerate for $1^1/2$ hours.
3 Pre-heat the oven, place the chicken on a roasting rack and cook for 15–17 minutes. When the juices run clear, the chicken is cooked.

Spatchcock in Vine Leaves

2 x No. 4 spatchcocks, halved
3 tbsp liquid honey
3 tbsp olive oil
3 tbsp orange juice
2 tsp lemon thyme, finely chopped
$^1/_2$ cup white wine
8–10 vine leaves

1 Rinse out the spatchcocks, and pat dry. Combine the honey, oil, juice, thyme and wine. Place the spatchcocks in a bowl and pour half the liquid over them. Cover and refrigerate, turning over 1–2 times over night.

2 Pre-heat the oven.
3 Wrap the spatchcocks in vine leaves and secure with skewers. Bake in a roasting dish for 25–30 minutes. Remove the leaves, and return the spatchcocks to the oven for 10 minutes (or until cooked and brown).
4 Remove the skewers, and place the spatchcocks on their leaves.
5 Heat the remaining marinade in a pan and pour it over the spatchcocks before serving.

OVEN TEMPERATURE
180°C, 350°F, GAS 4

Serves 2
Preparation 10mins plus refrigeration
Cooking 40mins
Calories 535
Fat 4.2g

Chicken with Ricotta, Rocket and Roasted Red capsicum

OVEN TEMPERATURE
200°C, 400°F, GAS 6

Serves 4
Preparation 10mins
Cooking 25mins
Calories 564
Fat 15.7g

200g/7oz fresh ricotta
1 cup rocket, roughly chopped
$^1/_4$ cup pinenuts, toasted
$^1/_2$ red capsicum, roasted and
finely chopped
freshly ground pepper and salt
4 chicken breasts, skin on;
each 170g–200g/6oz–7oz
4 tbsp butter
1 cup chicken stock

1 Preheat the oven.
2 Combine the ricotta, rocket, pinenuts, capsicum and pepper and salt in a small bowl and mix together until smooth.

3 Place 1–2 tablespoons of ricotta mixture under the skin of each chicken breast. Lightly grease a baking dish. Place the chicken breasts in the dish, sprinkle with pepper and salt, place 1 teaspoon of butter on each breast and pour the stock around the chicken. Bake, for 20–25 minutes.
4 Serve the chicken with pan-juices and an rocket salad.

Vindaloo Chicken Nuggets

900g/2 lb chicken thigh fillets
salt and pepper
1 tbsp lemon juice
2 tbsp vindaloo curry paste
1 cup flour
2 eggs, beaten
1¹/₂ cups dried breadcrumbs
canola oil spray

1 Cut each fillet into 4 pieces. Place in a bowl, sprinkle lightly with salt and pepper then pour over the lemon juice. Toss with a spoon to mix through. Rub the curry paste well into each piece with your fingers. Cover and refrigerate for 2 hours or more.

2 Coat the fillets with flour, egg and breadcrumbs as for schnitzels. Lightly spray a large flat tray with canola oil spray and place on the nuggets. Lightly spray the surface of the nuggets. Cook in a preheated oven for 15–18 minutes.

OVEN TEMPERATURE
180°C, 350°F, GAS 4

Serves 6
Preparation 15mins
Cooking 18mins
Calories 392
Fat 2.4g

Glossary

acidulated water: water with added acid, such as lemon juice or vinegar, which prevents discolouration of ingredients, particularly fruit or vegetables. The proportion of acid to water is 1 teaspoon per 300mL.

al dente: Italian cooking term for ingredients that are cooked until tender but still firm to the bite; usually applied to pasta.

americaine: method of serving seafood, usually lobster and monkfish, in a sauce flavoured with olive oil, aromatic herbs, tomatoes, white wine, fish stock, brandy and tarragon.

anglaise: cooking style for simple cooked dishes such as boiled vegetables. Assiette anglaise is a plate of cold cooked meats.

antipasto: Italian for 'before the meal', it denotes an assortment of cold meats, vegetables and cheeses, often marinated, served as an hors d'oeuvre. A typical antipasto might include salami, prosciutto, marinated artichoke hearts, anchovy fillets, olives, tuna fish and Provolone cheese.

au gratin: food sprinkled with breadcrumbs, often covered with cheese sauce and browned until a crisp coating forms.

balsamic vinegar: a mild, extremely fragrant, wine-based vinegar made in northern Italy. Traditionally, the vinegar is aged for at least seven years in a series of casks made of various woods.

baste: to moisten food while it is cooking by spooning or brushing on liquid or fat.

baine marie: a saucepan standing in a large pan which is filled with boiling water to keep liquids at simmering point. A double boiler will do the same job.

beat: to stir thoroughly and vigorously.

beurre manie: equal quantities of butter and flour kneaded together and added, a little at a time, to thicken a stew or casserole.

bird: see paupiette.

blanc: a cooking liquid made by adding flour and lemon juice to water in order to keep certain vegetables from discolouring as they cook.

blanch: to plunge into boiling water and then, in some cases, into cold water. Fruits and nuts are blanched to remove skin easily.

blanquette: a white stew of lamb, veal or chicken, bound with egg yolks and cream and accompanied by onion and mushrooms.

blend: to mix thoroughly.

bonne femme: dishes cooked in the traditional French 'housewife' style. Chicken and pork bonne femme are garnished with bacon, potatoes and baby onion; fish bonne femme with mushrooms in a white wine sauce.

bouquet garni: a bunch of herbs, usually consisting of sprigs of parsley, thyme, marjoram, rosemary, a bay leaf, peppercorns and cloves, tied in muslin and used to flavour stews and casseroles.

braise: to cook whole or large pieces of poultry, game, fish, meat or vegetables in a small amount of wine, stock or other liquid in a closed pot. Often the main ingredient is first browned in fat and then cooked in a low oven or very slowly on top of the stove. Braising suits tough meats and older birds and produces a mellow, rich sauce.

broil: the American term for grilling food.

brown: cook in a small amount of fat until brown.

burghul (also bulgur): a type of cracked wheat, where the kernels are steamed and dried before being crushed.

buttered: to spread with softened or melted butter.

butterfly: to slit a piece of food in half horizontally, cutting it almost through so that, when opened, it resembles butterfly wings. Chops, large prawns and thick fish fillets are often butterflied so that they cook more quickly.

buttermilk: a tangy, low-fat cultured milk product its slight acidity makes it an ideal marinade base for poultry.

calzone: a semicircular pocket of pizza dough, stuffed with meat or vegetables, sealed and baked.

caramelise: to melt sugar until it is a golden brown syrup.

champignons: small mushrooms, usually canned.

chasseur: (hunter) a French cooking style in which meat and chicken dishes are cooked with mushrooms, spring onions, white wine, and often tomato.

clarify: to melt butter and drain the oil off the sediment.

coat: to cover with a thin layer of flour, sugar, nuts, crumbs, poppy or sesame seeds, cinnamon sugar or a few of the ground spices.

concasser: to chop coarsely, usually tomatoes.

confit: from the French verb *confire*, meaning to preserve. Food that is made into a preserve by cooking very slowly and thoroughly until tender. In the case of meat, such as duck or goose, it is cooked in its own fat, and covered with the fat so that the meat does not come into contact with the air. Vegetables such as onions are good in confit.

consomme: a clear soup usually made from beef.

coulis: a thin puree, usually of fresh or cooked fruit or vegetables, which is soft enough to pour (couler means 'to run'). A coulis may be rough-textured or very smooth.

court bouillon: the liquid in which fish, poultry or meat is cooked. It usually consists of water with bay leaf, onion, carrots and salt and freshly ground black pepper to taste. Other additives may include wine, vinegar, stock, garlic or scallions (scallions).

couscous: cereal processed from semolina into pellets, traditionally steamed and served with meat and vegetables in the classic North African stew of the same name.

cruciferous vegetables: certain members of the mustard, cabbage and turnip families with cross-shaped flowers and strong aromas and flavours.

cream: to make soft, smooth and creamy by rubbing with the back of a spoon or by beating with a mixer. Usually applied to fat and sugar.

croutons: small toasted or fried cubes of bread.

crudites: raw vegetables, cut in slices or sticks to nibble plain or with a dipping sauce, or shredded vegetables tossed as salad with a simple dressing.

cube: to cut into small pieces with six equal sides.

curdle: to cause milk or sauce to separate into solid and liquid. Example, overcooked egg mixtures.

daikon radish: (also called mooli): a long white Japanese radish.

dark sesame oil (also called Oriental sesame oil): dark polyunsaturated oil with a low burning point, used for seasoning. Do not replace with lighter sesame oil.

deglaze: to dissolve congealed cooking juices or glaze on the bottom of a pan by adding a liquid, then scraping and stirring vigorously whilst bringing the liquid to the boil. Juices may be used to make gravy or to add to sauce.

degrease: to skim grease from the surface of liquid. If possible the liquid should be chilled so the fat solidifies. If not, skim off most of the fat with a large metal spoon, then trail strips of paper towel on the surface of the liquid to remove any remaining globules.

devilled: a dish or sauce that is highly seasoned with a hot ingredient such as mustard, Worcestershire sauce or cayenne pepper.

dice: to cut into small cubes.

dietary fibre: a plant-cell material that is undigested or only partially digested in the human body, but which promotes healthy digestion of other food matter.

dissolve: mix a dry ingredient with liquid until absorbed.

dredge: to coat with a dry ingredient, as flour or sugar.

drizzle: to pour in a fine thread-like stream over a surface.

dust: to sprinkle or coat lightly with flour or icing sugar.

Dutch oven: a heavy casserole with a lid usually made from cast iron or pottery.

emulsion: a mixture of two liquids that are not mutually soluble-for example, oil and water.

entree: in Europe, the 'entry' or hors d'oeuvre; in North America entree means the main course.

fillet: special cut of beef, lamb, pork or veal; breast of poultry and game; fish cut off the bone lengthways.

flake: to break into small pieces with a fork.

flame: to ignite warmed alcohol over food.

fold in: a gentle, careful combining of a light or delicate mixture with a heavier mixture, using a metal spoon.

fricassee: a dish in which poultry, fish or vegetables are bound together with a white or veloute sauce. In Britain and the United States, the name applies to an old-fashioned dish of chicken in a creamy sauce.

galette: sweet or savoury mixture shaped as a flat round.

garnish: to decorate food, usually with something edible.

gastrique: caramelized sugar deglazed with vinegar and used in fruit-flavoured savoury sauces, in such dishes as duck with orange.

glaze: a thin coating of beaten egg, syrup or aspic which is brushed over pastry, fruits or cooked meats.

gluten: a protein in flour that is developed when dough is kneaded, making the dough elastic.

gratin: a dish cooked in the oven or under the grill so that it develops a brown crust. Breadcrumbs or cheese may be sprinkled on top first. Shallow gratin dishes ensure a maximum area of crust.

grease: to rub or brush lightly with oil or fat.

joint: to cut poultry, game or small animals into serving pieces by dividing at the joint.

julienne: to cut food into match-like strips.

knead: to work dough using heel of hand with a pressing motion, while stretching and folding the dough.

line: to cover the inside of a container with paper, to protect or aid in removing mixture.

infuse: to immerse herbs, spices or other flavourings in hot liquid to flavour it. Infusion takes from 2-5 minutes depending on the flavouring. The liquid should be very hot but not boiling.

jardiniere: a garnish of garden vegetables, typically carrots, pickling onions, French beans and turnips.

lights: lungs of an animal, used in various meat preparations such as pâtés and faggots.

macerate: to soak food in liquid to soften.

marinade: a seasoned liquid, usually an oil and acid mixture, in which meats or other foods are soaked to soften and give more flavour.

marinara: Italian 'sailor's style' cooking that does not apply to any particular combination of ingredients. Marinara tomato sauce for pasta is the most familiar.

marinate: to let food stand in a marinade to season and tenderize.

mask: to cover cooked food with sauce.

melt: to heat until liquified.

mince: to grind into very small pieces.

mix: to combine ingredients by stirring.

monounsaturated fats: one of three types of fats found in foods. Are believed not to raise the level of cholesterol in the blood.

nicoise: a garnish of tomatoes, garlic and black olives; a salad with anchovy, tuna and French beans is typical.

non-reactive pan: a cooking pan whose surface does not chemically react with food. Materials used include stainless steel, enamel, glass and some alloys.

noisette: small 'nut' of lamb cut from boned loin or rack that is rolled, tied and cut in neat slices. Noisette also means flavoured with hazelnuts, or butter cooked to a nut brown colour.

normande: a cooking style for fish, with a garnish of prawn, mussels and mushrooms in a white wine cream sauce; for poultry and meat, a sauce with cream, calvados and apple.

olive oil: various grades of oil extracted from olives. Extra virgin olive oil has a full, fruity flavour and the lowest acidity. Virgin olive oil is slightly higher in acidity and lighter in flavour. Pure olive oil is a processed blend of olive oils and has the highest acidity and lightest taste.

panade: a mixture for binding stuffings and dumplings, notably quenelles, often of choux pastry or simply breadcrumbs. A panade may also be made of frangipane, pureed potatoes or rice.

papillote: to cook food in oiled or buttered greaseproof paper or aluminum foil. Also a decorative frill to cover bone ends of chops and poultry drumsticks.

parboil: to boil or simmer until part cooked (i.e. cooked further than when blanching).

pare: to cut away outside covering.

pate: a paste of meat or seafood used as a spread for toast or crackers.

paupiette: a thin slice of meat, poultry or fish spread with a savoury stuffing and rolled. In the United States this is also called 'bird' and in Britain an 'olive'.

peel: to strip away outside covering.

plump: to soak in liquid or moisten thoroughly until full and round.

poach: to simmer gently in enough hot liquid to cover, using care to retain shape of food.

polyunsaturated fat: one of the three types of fats found in food. These exist in large quantities in such vegetable oils as safflower, sunflower, corn and soya bean. These fats lower the level of cholesterol in the blood.

puree: a smooth paste, usually of vegetables or fruits, made by putting foods through a sieve, food mill or liquefying in a blender or food processor.

ragout: traditionally a well seasoned, rich stew containing meat, vegetables and wine. Nowadays, a term applied to any stewed mixture.

ramekins: small oval or round individual baking dishes.

reconstitute: to put moisture back into dehydrated foods by soaking in liquid.

reduce: to cook over a very high heat, uncovered, until the liquid is reduced by evaporation.

refresh: to cool hot food quickly, either under running water or by plunging it into iced water, to stop it cooking. Particularly for

vegetables and occasionally for shellfish.

rice vinegar: mild, fragrant vinegar that is less sweet than cider vinegar and not as harsh as distilled malt vinegar. Japanese rice vinegar is milder than the Chinese variety.

roulade: a piece of meat, usually pork or veal, that is spread with stuffing, rolled and often braised or poached. A roulade may also be a sweet or savoury mixture that is baked in a Swiss roll tin or paper case, filled with a contrasting filling, and rolled.

rubbing-in: a method of incorporating fat into flour, by use of fingertips only. Also incorporates air into mixture.

safflower oil: the vegetable oil that contains the highest proportion of polyunsaturated fats.

salsa: a juice derived from the main ingredient being cooked, or a sauce added to a dish to enhance its flavour. In Italy the term is often used for pasta sauces; in Mexico the name usually applies to uncooked sauces served as an accompaniment, especially to corn chips.

saturated fats: one of the three types of fats found in foods. These exist in large quantities in animal products, coconut and palm oils; they raise the level of cholesterol in the blood. As high cholesterol levels may cause heart disease, saturated fat consumption is recommended to be less than 15 percent of calories provided by the daily diet.

sauté: to cook or brown in small amount of hot fat.

score: to mark food with cuts, notches or lines to prevent curling or to make food more attractive.

scald: to bring just to boiling point, usually for milk. Also to rinse with boiling water.

sear: to brown surface quickly over high heat in hot dish.

seasoned flour: flour with salt and pepper added.

sift: to shake a dry, powdered substance through a sieve or sifter to remove any lumps and give lightness.

simmer: to cook food gently in liquid that bubbles steadily just below boiling point so that the food cooks in even heat without breaking up.

singe: to quickly flame poultry to remove all traces of feathers after plucking.

skim: to remove a surface layer (often of impurities and scum) from a liquid with a metal spoon or small ladle.

slivered: sliced in long, thin pieces, usually refers to nuts, especially almonds.

soften: example: gelatine - sprinkle over cold water and allow to gel (soften) then dissolve and liquefy.

souse: to cover food, particularly fish, in wine vinegar and spices and cook slowly; the food is cooled in the same liquid. Sousing gives food a pickled flavour.

steep: to soak in warm or cold liquid in order to soften food and draw out strong flavours or impurities.

stir-fry: to cook thin slices of meat and vegetable over a high heat in a small amount of oil, stirring constantly to even cooking in a short time. Traditionally cooked in a wok, however a heavy-based frying pan may be used.

stock: a liquid containing flavours, extracts and nutrients of bones, meat, fish or vegetables.

stud: to adorn with; for example, baked ham studded with whole cloves.

sweat: to cook vegetables over heat until only juices run.

sugo: an Italian sauce made from the liquid or juice extracted from fruit or meat during cooking.

sweat: to cook sliced or chopped food, usually vegetables, in a little fat and no liquid over very low heat. Foil is pressed on top so that the food steams in its own juices, usually before being added to other dishes.

timbale: a creamy mixture of vegetables or meat baked in a mould. French for 'kettledrum'; also denotes a drum-shaped baking dish.

thicken: to make a thin, smooth paste by mixing together arrowroot, cornflour or flour with an equal amount of cold water; stir into hot liquid, cook, stirring until thickened.

toss: to gently mix ingredients with two forks or fork and spoon.

total fat: the individual daily intake of all three fats previously described in this glossary. Nutritionists recommend that fats provide no more than 35percent of the energy in the diet.

vine leaves: tender, lightly flavoured leaves of the grapevine, used in ethnic cuisine as wrappers for savoury mixtures. As the leaves are usually packed in brine, they should be well rinsed before use.

whip: to beat rapidly, incorporate air and produce expansion.

zest: thin outer layer of citrus fruits containing the aromatic citrus oil. It is usually thinly pared with a vegetable peeler, or grated with a zester or grater to separate it from the bitter white pith underneath.

Weights and Measures

Cooking is not an exact science; one does not require finely calibrated scales, pipettes and scientific equipment to cook, yet the conversion to metric measures in some countries and its interpretations must have intimidated many a good cook.

In the recipes weights are given for ingredients such as meats, fish, poultry and some vegetables, but in normal cooking a few ounces or grams one way or another will not affect the success of your dish.

Allthough recipes have been tested using the Australian Standard 250mL cup, 20mL tablespoon and 5mL teaspoon, they will work just as well with the US and Canadian 8fl oz cup, or the UK 300mL cup. We have used graduated cup measures in preference to tablespoon measures so that proportions are always the same. Where tablespoon measures have been given, they are not crucial measures, so using the smaller tablespoon of the US or UK will not affect the recipe's success. At least we all agree on the teaspoon size.

For breads, cakes and pastries, the only area which might cause concern is where eggs are used, as proportions will then vary. If working with a 250mL or 300mL cup, use large eggs (65g/2^1/$_4$ oz), adding a little more liquid to the recipe for 300mL cup measures if it seems necessary. Use the medium-sized eggs (55g/2oz) with 8fl oz cup measure. A graduated set of measuring cups and spoons is recommended, the cups in particular for measuring dry ingredients. Remember to level such ingredients to ensure an accurate quantity.

English Measures

All measurements are similar to Australian with two exceptions: the English cup measures 300mL/10^1/$_2$ fl oz, whereas the American and Australian cup measure 250mL/8^3/$_4$ fl oz. The English tablespoon (the Australian dessertspoon) measures 14.8mL /1^1/$_2$ fl oz against Australian tablespoon of 20mL/^{3}/$_4$ fl oz. The Imperial measurement is 20fl oz to the pint, 40fl oz a quart and 160fl oz one gallon.

American Measures

The American reputed pint is 16fl oz, a quart is equal to 32fl oz and the American gallon, 128fl oz. The American tablespoon is equal to 14.8mL/^{1}/$_2$ fl oz, the teaspoon is 5mL/^{1}/$_6$ fl oz. The cup measure is 250 mL/8^3/$_4$ fl oz.

Dry Measures

All the measures are level, so when you have filled a cup or spoon, level it off with the edge of a knife. The scale below is the 'cook's equivalent'; it is not an exact conversion of metric to imperial measurement. To calculate the exact metric equivalent yourself, multiply onces x 28.349523 to obtain grams, or divide 28.349523 grams to obtain onces.

Metric	Imperial
g = grams	oz = ounces
kg = kilograms	lb = pound
15g	^{1}/$_2$ oz
20g	^{2}/$_3$ oz
30g	1oz
55g	2oz
85g	3oz
115g	4oz/^{1}/$_4$ lb
125g	4^1/$_2$ oz
140/145g	5oz
170g	6oz
200g	7oz
225g	8oz/^{1}/$_2$ lb
315g	11oz
340g	12oz/^{3}/$_4$ lb
370g	13oz
400g	14oz
425g	15oz
455g	16oz/1 lb
1,000g/1kg	35.3oz/2.2 lb
1.5kg	3.33 lb

Oven Temperatures

The Celsius temperatures given here are not exact; they have been rounded off and are given as a guide only. Follow the manufacturer's temperature guide, relating it to oven description given in the recipe. Remember gas ovens are hottest at the top, electric ovens at the bottom and convection-fan forced ovens are usually even throughout. We included Regulo numbers for gas cookers which may assist. To convert °C to °F multiply °C by 9 and divide by 5 then add 32.

Oven Temperatures

	C°	F°	Gas regulo
Very slow	120	250	1
Slow	150	300	2
Moderately slow	160	325	3
Moderate	180	350	4
Moderately hot	190–200	370–400	5–6
Hot	210–220	410–440	6–7
Very hot	230	450	8
Super hot	250–290	475–500	9–10

Cake Dish Sizes

metric	imperial
15cm	6in
18cm	7in
20cm	8in
23cm	9in

Loaf Dish Sizes

metric	imperial
23 x 12cm	9 x 5in
25 x 8cm	10 x 3in
28 x 18cm	11 x 7in

Liquid Measures

metric	imperial	cup and spoon
mL	fl oz	
millilitres	fluid ounce	
5mL	$1/6$ fl oz	1 teaspoon
20mL	$2/3$ fl oz	1 tablespoon
30mL	1 fl oz	1 tbsp + 2 tsp
55mL	2 fl oz	
63mL	$2^1/4$ fl oz	$1/4$ cup
85mL	3 fl oz	
115mL	4 fl oz	
125mL	$4^1/2$ fl oz	$1/2$ cup
150mL	$5^1/4$ fl oz	
188mL	$6^2/3$ fl oz	$3/4$ cup
225mL	8 fl oz	
250mL	$8^3/4$ fl oz	1 cup
300mL	$10^1/2$ fl oz	
370mL	13 fl oz	
400mL	14 fl oz	
438mL	$15^1/2$ fl oz	$1^3/4$ cups
455mL	16 fl oz	
500mL	$17^1/2$ fl oz	2 cups
570mL	20 fl oz	
1 litre	35.3 fl oz	4 cups

Cup Measurements

One cup is equal to the following weights.

	Metric	Imperial
Almonds, flaked	85g	3oz
Almonds, slivered, ground	125g	$4^1/2$ oz
Almonds, kernel	155g	$5^1/2$ oz
Apples, dried, chopped	125g	$4^1/2$ oz

	Metric	Imperial
Apricots, dried, chopped	190g	$6^3/4$ oz
Breadcrumbs, packet	125g	$4^1/2$ oz
Breadcrumbs, soft	55g	2oz
Cheese, grated	115g	4oz
Choc bits	$155^1/2$ g	5oz
Coconut, desiccated	90g	3oz
Cornflakes	30g	1oz
Currants	$155^1/2$ g	5oz
Flour	115g	4oz
Fruit, dried (mixed, sultanas etc)	170g	6 oz
Ginger, crystallised, glace	250g	8oz
Honey, treacle, golden syrup	315g	11oz
Mixed peel	225g	8oz
Nuts, chopped	115g	4oz
Prunes, chopped	225g	8oz
Rice, cooked	155g	$5^1/2$ oz
Rice, uncooked	225g	8oz
Rolled oats	90g	3oz
Sesame seeds	115g	4oz
Shortening (butter, margarine)	225g	8oz
Sugar, brown	155g	$5^1/2$ oz
Sugar, granulated or caster	225g	8oz
Sugar, sifted icing	155g	$5^1/2$ oz
Wheatgerm	60g	2oz

Length

Some of us still have trouble converting imperial length to metric. In this scale, measures have been rounded off to the easiest-to-use and most acceptable figures. To obtain the exact metric equivalent in converting inches to centimetres, multiply inches by 2.54 whereby 1 inch equals 25.4 millimetres and 1 millimetre equals 0.03937 inches.

Metric	Imperial
mm=millimetres	in = inches
cm=centimetres	ft = feet
5mm, 0.5cm	$1/4$ in
10mm, 1.0cm	$1/2$ in
20mm, 2.0cm	$3/4$ in
2.5cm	1in
5 cm	2in
$7^1/2$ cm	3in
10cm	4in
$12^1/2$ cm	5in
15cm	6in
18cm	7in
20cm	8in
23cm	9in
25cm	10in
28cm	11in
30cm	12in, 1 foot

Index

Apricot glazed chicken with savoury stuffing 60

Asian chicken and kaffir lime salad 41

Asian marinated chicken drumsticks 71

Australian-style chicken curry 56

Cajun chicken brochettes 27

Chicken and almond triangles 11

Chicken and endive salad with creamy dressing 30

Chicken and prune roll 12

Chicken caesar salad 32

Chicken focaccia with marinated vegetables 13

Chicken in a crust **9**

Chicken in a pan **43**

Chicken in a salad **29**

Chicken in an oven **59**

Chicken kebabs with couscous 26

Chicken leek and mushroom flan 14

Chicken minestrone 57

Chicken on a grill **21**

Chicken pitta 15

Chicken rolls with an Indonesian flavour 52

Chicken Waldorf 31

Chicken wings Moroccan style 53

Chicken with ricotta, rocket and
  roasted red capsicum 74

Citrus and spice grilled chicken 22

Crunchy chicken and potato salad 34

Crunchy drumsticks 62

Curried chicken rolls 16

Curried chicken salad 35

Easy apricot and mango chicken loaf 63

Glossary **76**

Grilled sesame chicken with ginger rice 24

Hawaiian poached chicken 54

Introduction **4**

Italian chicken in a pan 46

Lavash rolls 17

Malaysian grilled chicken 25

Marinated chicken salad 47

Middle Eastern chicken pasties 10

No-fuss chicken party sticks 18

Orange and spice leg steaks 48

Oven baked chicken schnitzels 64

Oven-baked Parmesan chicken 69

Party avocado and chicken salad 38

Poached chicken with tomato
  and mushroom sauce 55

Quick chicken lasagne 65

Risotto of Indian spiced chicken with chickpeas 50

Roast chicken with basil and red onion 68

Roasted herb stuffed chicken (kota yemista) 72

Roasted herby chicken with pears 70

Satay wings for a crowd 66

Southern barbecued chicken 23

Spatchcock in vine leaves 73

Spicy chicken burritos 19

Tandoori chicken 67

Tandoori chicken pockets 44

Tangy tenderloins 49

Tossed greens and chicken with
  blue cheese dressing 39

Tropical chicken salad 40

Warm salad of mustard-glazed chicken
  with red wine vinaigrette 36

Weights and measures **76**